DAZE OF ISOLATION

••••••••••••••••••••

SURVIVING PANDEMIC MOTHERHOOD ON
DIET COKE AND A PRAYER

KRISTA EHLERS

Rough Cut Publishing
MILL CREEK, WA

Copyright © 2021 by Krista Ehlers.

All rights reserved. No part of this publication may be reproduced, distributed or transmitted in any form or by any means, including photocopying, recording, or other electronic or mechanical methods, without the prior written permission of the publisher, except in the case of brief quotations embodied in critical reviews and certain other noncommercial uses permitted by copyright law. For permission requests, write to the publisher, addressed "Attention: Permissions Coordinator," at the address below.

Krista Ehlers/Rough Cut Publishing
PO Box 12301
Mill Creek, WA 98082
www.roughcutpublishing.com

Book Layout ©2017 BookDesignTemplates.com

Daze of Isolation/ Krista Ehlers. -- 1st ed.
ISBN 978-1-7374733-4-3

CONTENTS

Countdown 7
March 11
April 27
May 53
June 71
July 89
August 111
September 131
October 149
November 167
December 185
January 203
February 219
March. Again. 237
Epilogue 249

*Dedicated to my husband,
who puts up with a lot.*

COUNTDOWN

●●●●●●●●●●●●●●●●●●●●●

When did the novel Coronavirus first hit your radar? One day my husband, Jeff, read me dire predictions from China, and weeks later, the first U.S. case cropped up about 10 miles from our house. Less than a month after that, Costco ran out of toilet paper.

Within the week, our school district became the first in the nation to close down and jump ship to online learning. Without warning, my 8th grade son, Damien, and 2nd grade daughter, Mary, came home indefinitely and I turned into a reluctant home-school mom.

I panicked: My two little bundles of joy both came with ADHD pre-installed, as well as some so-called co-morbid conditions. I depended on them being in school to support our family's sanity. My husband came home from the office in mid-February and never went back. What would I do with all of us home? All day? Every day?

Well, go insane, of course. We knuckled down and got creative, but some ideas were more successful than others. Morning walks with Mary got some wiggles out, though she revolted midway through shutdown, and I continued alone. Friday night pizza and a movie were a well-received, but Saturday morning family walks were like pulling teeth. Sunday afternoon drives were hit and miss: the destinations were popular, but the hours packed in the car together strained our collective nerves.

Surviving Pandemic Motherhood on Diet Coke and a Prayer

I started writing a daily Facebook post to chronicle these unprecedented events, to sort out my feelings and to exchange support with friends: all of us going through the same thing, each in our distinct ways. Those posts turned into this book, and some of my friends' comments make guest appearances. Patricia, Sue, Amber and the rest of the gang all pop up from time to time.

What was supposed to be a two-week school closure stretched beyond a year, and those last days before shutdown now take on the tone of a "countdown to launch" of isolation.

T minus Three

Three days before our district closed, the superintendent gave parents the option to keep students home if we deemed it unsafe to send them to school. Mine went. Both kids reported that half their classmates stayed home. Mary missed the other students; Damien envied his friends for sleeping in.

I studied a number of articles about the Coronavirus, and I concluded that the virus itself is unlikely to kill me. However, the steps to contain the virus' spread, may, in fact, kill me.

T minus Two

Two days before shutdown, all schools in the area paused for a deep cleaning. Sorta' like a snow day, only no sparkly snow, and with nagging concern about where this was all going.

Mary: Mom! I have a good idea... Put on some *rock* music.

Me, to self: Aw, heck, yeah!

It was that kind of day.

T minus One

One day before shutdown, reports came from near and far about people's bizarre reactions to pandemic stress. One shopper in Australia drew a knife in a fight over toilet paper![1]

Steps for Coronavirus safety:
1. Wash your hands.
2. Don't touch your face.
3. Don't take TP from someone else's cart.

Blast off!

Late on a Wednesday night, we got the news that our district would shut down. The virus was encroaching on our town, from the first case 10 miles north and the first deaths 8 miles south. Though the writing was on the wall, the message was still shocking.

Welp, our school district shut down for the next fourteen days. F o u r t e e n . I'm trying not to freak out. But when they were home Tuesday, we had a 90-minute power struggle over *one* worksheet! Today, my 2nd grader came home with *forty* worksheets. Damien grumbled about how boring school was this week. I warned, "Wait until you experience the School of Mom!" Keep it together, keep it together, keep it together...

---

[1] See https://www.mirror.co.uk/news/world-news/shopper-draws-knife-fight-over-21627926

MARCH

NON-MARCHING ORDERS

We were all in shock. They can close schools? With electricity on and without snow? After they sent the children home, people gave me lots of advice about taking my kids to the library and the zoo and trampoline parks. That may or may not have worked, but the point was moot. By the end of March, those places were all closed as well. Soon, there was nowhere to go but select stores and restaurant drive-thrus.

● ● ● ● ● ● ● ● ● ● ● ● ● ● ● ● ● ● ●

Day 1 of Isolation

Our first day of isolation started with leaving the house ASAP to go for a walk with Grandma. We called that "P.E." We had breakfast from McDonald's on the way, which we called, "supporting our troubled economy." Checked at Costco again for TP - they were still out. Stopped at McDonald's again for Diet Coke on the way home, since I saved $23.99 by not getting toilet paper at Costco, which I chose to call "Math." And this is how we will muddle through.

Day 2 of Isolation

No heads were bitten off by Mom until 4:35 PM today, and it was only one head rather than all the heads. Not even a bitten off, really: more of a graze. Don't expect this kind of self-control every day, mind you. Teachers clearly went easy on us these first two days. In other news, I got a reassuring, jumbo package of TP at Fred Meyer this morning, with no weapons. Damien made dinner. Things shaped up nicely, all things considered.

Accidental Homeschooler's FAQ
Q: How do I make the children settle down and do the school? (Because my daughter is 90% jumping bean.)
A: Bribes.
Q: How do I accomplish anything during school that is not school?
A: I don't.
Q: How do I deal with extra needs like ADHD, autism spectrum, ODD, PTSD, anxiety, OCD…?
A: Refined sugar and Diet Coke. Repeat.

#momoftheyear

Day 3 of Isolation

I haven't been this relieved to greet Saturday since high school! The kids and I had no school and Jeff had no work, and we could do our usual thing: LA Fitness, McDonald's, haircuts for all, nap for Dad, nap for Mom, Denny's pancakes for supper. So pleasant. In fact, I bet you're a little envious of our rockin' Saturday.

We all needed the rest. Mary *yawned* during the last lesson on both days so far, which was when I realized I had never seen her yawn before. Damien commented that he thinks this was harder than regular school. That was disturbing, because this week was "practice;" the full workload would start tomorrow. Deep breaths…

Day 4 of Isolation

Church, where we all lathered up with hand sanitizer and greeted each other in non-touchy ways. People: can we agree to *not* let the Elbow Bump become a thing? So undignified! Grown men and women using a karate move as a greeting! Let us wave or virtual high five or how about bowing? Japan made that work for thousands of years...

In the afternoon, we puttered about the house, followed by food and Skip-Bo at Jack in the Box. It's becoming apparent that one thing I do poorly in my days of isolation is the isolating. I need my freedom! And we're not sick. And I'm weak. I vow to wash my hands a *lot*.

Day 5 of Isolation

Let the record show that the children lasted eleven minutes before fisticuffs erupted in the kitchen. First full day of online learning was a bust. Imma' just pretend school starts tomorrow. Mary's half-hour math lesson dragged out to mid-afternoon. I "sent" Damien to the wrong class for electives, so he was marked... what? eTruant?

Later, in a cruel twist of fate, our doctor gave us the wrong appointment time. So, my stir-crazy kids were trapped in the doctor's lobby for two hours.

Let's wad this day up like a piece of paper, toss it in the bin, and pretend it never happened. Where's the chocolate?

I confess: a few things went well. I arranged a school computer for Mary. Now the kids don't squabble over the only device that runs i-Ready. Mary insisted on doing PE *at* our gym, so she lugged her laptop into Kids Club. She says one of the caregivers did online PE with her. If I could've been a fly on that wall....

The sun smiled on us, and Jeff took me out to eat, so no cooking and lots of Diet Coke. Hey! I didn't finish that last soda. An only-slightly-flat Diet Coke is hiding in this house! Where'd that go...?

Day 6 of Isolation

Aaaaand I'm in tears. It was only a matter of time until this broke me.

Day 7 of Isolation

I wish I could say today was better than yesterday, but not so much. I forgot to have lunch because I was busy ugly crying in my room while Jeff took over meltdown duty. Which means now we're both exhausted.

But I reached out for help, at home and with the teachers, and God provided in so many ways.

- Washed my hair and snuck in a nap.
- Teacher Zoom call = 30 minutes of happy daughter.
- Occupational Therapy still open = 50 minutes of peace.
- Sunshine (in Seattle, sunshine is an event.)
- Son finished school early and did chores (score!)
- Tax refund came today.
- Friend left bubble bath and pastries on our porch.
- Church still open = warm meal and listening ears!
- Kids Club and gym still open = P.E. done!
- McDonald's was still open = Diet Coke breaks.

So, we are getting through this. Lots of schools around here shut down today, and to you I say, "We'll get through this together."

Daze of Isolation

The LA Fitness parking lot was barren this morning, which was excellent because that left fewer people to witness me drinking my large Diet Coke while working out. Not even kidding. I'm sinking to new lows.

Day 8 of Isolation

I thought we were getting the hang of this. We nearly completed school today, and without meltdowns! Last night, the governor shut down Seattle/Tacoma schools until April 24. Thus, most districts moved to online learning. Not our district. They did the *opposite*, putting online learning "on pause" for who knows how long. Students still won't be allowed in the building, but there won't be any lessons, either. So... I mean... What will my kids do for 6 weeks? Start summer early, only with no camps, and lots of rain? I just... All that effort to shoehorn the children into a routine... and now, nothing?

Day 9 of Isolation

This morning, we walked past Daddy's bus stop. This landmark was made famous in the Ehlers family because we picked up our favorite Daddy here sometimes when he got off work. By the time we got there, Mary was wearing my ear band over her mouth. Not to keep out germs, but because her lips were cold. What about my ears, you say? Well, they got cold, as you can imagine. Next time: two ear bands.

Phrases I'm sick of hearing...
- abundance of caution
- rapidly evolving situation
- social distancing
- closely monitoring

- these unprecedented times
- your health and safety is our top priority

New things that closed today:

The Library. This one's gonna cost me — Damien and I are 100% Kindle, but Jeff and Mary still read paper books.

Broadway. Won't affect us much.

Disneyland/World. Same.

All the schools in Washington.

Cloud Learning 1.0. The 2nd graders said "bye" to each other on their Zoom lesson this morning, not knowing whether they'd meet again — I almost teared up! Side note: 2nd graders on videoconference was super adorable.

> **Jeff, finishing work:** What's the plan for supper?
>
> **Me, plopping down to rest:** I'm considering making Daddy Beef Stew, but.... Well, it's a rapidly evolving situation.

Day 10 of Isolation

Many of my friends and I are practicing what we in the biz call "Extreme Parenting." That is, we are parents of extreme kids. This term covers behavioral issues, learning delays, medical fragility, and all combinations thereof. They're weathering one or more of the "D's" — ADHD, LD, CHD, OCD, ASD, ODD, PTSD, RAD, SPD....

If you parent of an extreme child, you know. If you don't parent extreme kids, you may not believe in the concept. We still love you, but we may not have lengthy talks about parenting. Here's the rub: these parents count on an ample team of professional and peer support to survive each day without violence, property damage, and/or emergency room visits. No, I'm not exaggerating. And now, these kids are home from school with none of their supports available.

Actual responses from Extreme Parents:

- The only time I get a break is when they're at school.
- I'm legit scared.
- This is literally my worst nightmare.
- It's the only time I felt panic over the virus.

Extreme Parents, please meet my friends, Prayer Warriors. Even as they're reading, they ache to do something. They may, in fact, be murmuring a few words of prayer for you *right* now.

Prayer Warriors, please pray for these men and women, as God brings them to your mind. Their kids, like all kids, will act up from the change in routine, from cabin fever, from anxiety. Their acting up, however, is likely to be more extreme. Thank you!

Day 11 of Isolation

Damien was planning to catch a movie with buddies for his birthday, when the theaters stopped operations. We compensated for his loss with a week of surprises. First day: Shamrock shakes at McDonald's. Also, our last day of sitting inside a restaurant for many months. Other treats included Red Robin takeout, complete with birthday song; a surprise balloon avalanche, ice cream cake, and ordering an entire large pizza for him. He seemed mollified.

Day 12 of Isolation

Governor is closing restaurants, except drive-thru. Gatherings of more than fifty people are prohibited, which suggests that our gym is right out. All this forces me to admit that I am like a shark: I am compelled to move about my city, so I don't eat my children.

Surviving Pandemic Motherhood on Diet Coke and a Prayer

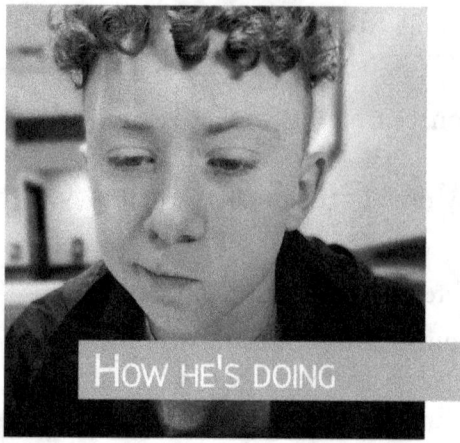

> **My mom:** How is Damien doing with all the closures?
>
> **Me:** Let me ask him
>
> **Damien:** Take a picture.

Day 13 of Isolation

The thing is, I embrace the quality of my homeschooling. I'm either doing well or doing the best I can, depending on time of day and Diet Coke accessibility. What I can't solve is how homeschool moms carve out *any* time to themselves to rest, catch up on urgent email/calendar/bills, shower, complete a sentence...

I may have figured something out: you sit at the computer and ignore the whiny voice asking you the same thing over and over. As necessary, repeat: "No, you cannot have screen time until your school is done." I'm calling this "Teacher In-Service Day."

Day 14 of Isolation

I cleaned my house. Regular cleaning was long overdue. Plus, corona cooties. So: deep clean. My house was built in 1996, and some places I sanitized today had not been addressed in twenty-four years. Since I was cleaning light switch plates and doorknobs,

Daze of Isolation

I figured I may as well wash the whole door. The door between the house and garage was the worst. Many other doors were bad. I won't tell you whose, to protect the identities of minors, and also you can't compel me to testify against my husband...

Day 15 of Isolation

Today, we did something eagerly anticipated by all parties: unlimited screen time! Expected results for the teen: he lay curled around his phone most of the day. Unexpected results from 8-year-old: she barely touched her Kindle and continues to make intense demands up on us. *Why won't she exercise her rights?*

By 9:30 AM, I was so discouraged, beat-up and angry that I took the two of us for a walk, in which I put loud music on my headphones. I think Jesus hand-picked the playlist:[2]

> Have you ever had one of those days, when nothing really goes your way? You got this.
>
> I'm forever on your side... my love? It knows no end.
>
> Miracles just happen like that.
>
> Hallelujah, *happy* day!

And a miracle *did* happen like that, because the Jesus playlist revived me. I could smile and enjoy my kid and the sunshine and ride out the rest of today.

---

[2] *You Got This*, by Love & the Outcome; *Forever on Your Side*, by Need to Breathe; *Miracles*, by Colton Dixon; *Happy Day*, by Crowder

Day 16 of Isolation

What's working?

The weather! This sunshine is boosting our spirits. Yes, Jeff told me the forecast. No, don't remind me. Trying ta' keep this swear-word free....

Walking, walking, walking. Or Basketball, if you're Damien. You'd think I'd be super svelte after all that exercising, but not so much, because what's also working is eating, eating, eating. So far, Mary is making 25¢ a day on our walks, finding loose change. No motivation problems getting her to do PE.

Wearing my clothes two days in a row. Who's gonna notice, McDonald's drive-thru staff? They will not rat me out. You all won't tell, because we're friends, and friends don't make friends do laundry.

Driving around traffic circles again and again. Well, it works for me — the other drivers who had to yield to me weren't so thrilled, so I only scored one revolution this morning.

80s hair metal bands. What could be more appropriate than head-banging music in these trying times? I find those songs strangely nostalgic. Strange because I wasn't a fan of them when they came out. But now, to my high school classmates with Def Leppard and Ratt scrawled on their binders, a hearty metal horns salute!

Getting up when Mary gets up. You can't imagine how much it pains me to do this, but the best days so far were the ones where I got up at 6:30 or whenever she came in. If she later balked at doing something I asked of her (e.g. school, chores), I said, "I'll go back to sleep, then." Bam! Cooperation.

Blaming anything bad that happens on the virus.

Broken down ice maker? Coronavirus

Jeff dropped the vacuum down the stairs? Coronavirus.
Bedroom lamp bulbs that burnt out months ago? Coronavirus.
Take that, Coronavirus!

Day 17 of Isolation

I've been voted "Most Likely to Be Quarantined" by a jury of my peers. Something about not washing my clothes often enough. Also, does the twenty seconds of handwashing seem like forever to anyone else?

Day 18 of Isolation

I think, "My daughter is so weird," because she insists on mounting some concrete stairs wearing rollerblades. Of course, I stand bundled up in hat, scarf, and gloves, while juggling an ice-cold Diet Coke to snap a picture of her. So...

Day 19 of Isolation

According to our district's initial announcement, my children should be seated cheerfully at their desks, in their classroom, with their teacher, but they're not. Forty-six states have now closed their schools, but reopening dates are all over the place. I'm guessing superintendents threw darts at a calendar. Kansas is the only state which preemptively shut down for the rest of the academic year. Those guys are brave. The other governors are hoping if they extend the closures little by little, the parents won't mutiny.

Day 20 of Isolation

There are two of me.
One of me recognizes that my discomfort and pain are caused by remaining in a house I love, with people I love, and I feel ashamed. Other families are at high risk of death due to age and/or

health issues. Some parents are doing triple duty: they work outside or inside home, school the kids, run the household. Some parents are "parent," without anyone else to take a shift. Some people wonder how they will finance their pandemic because they're not allowed to work at all. Some people are sick.

The other me dreads the days yawning out in front of me with no structure save what I cobble together. My youngest is relentless. I can't pick my battles because everything is a battle. That's not new, but school gave me a rest between battles. Now: no rest. No sooner do I set her on the right track, than one of my other people [naturally] ask me for something. Because they think that I'm "not doing anything." Which is fair, I guess, but still.

Somewhere in between these two of me is where I live my days. I wake up, I try not to grouse at my people. I try to check tasks off my list. I count on the kids going to sleep, when Jeff and I can sprawl in our bed, watching "our show," and enjoying our treat. Now showing: Netflix' "Lost in Space", hot cocoa, and Chobani Flip Salted Caramel Crunch. T minus 10 hours and 38 minutes.

Day 21 of Isolation

I wonder if we could swing take-out every night. Well, our budget could cover *me*, but for Jeff and the kids, too?

Barring that, I'm back to planning my grocery adventure for the week.

Every Wednesday, I look forward to the arrival of the Fred Meyer ad. At this point, grocery trips are thrilling. Supply chain delays and pandemic hoarding mean that my shopping list is unlikely to be fulfilled, but I don't care. Shopping gives me a legal excuse to go out! As if the latest sale flyer is not exciting enough,

McDonald's "Buy One, Get One Free Happy Meal" coupon is in their app.

> **Tara:** *downloads McDonald's app*
>
> **Karla:** I was standing in Walgreens today thinking how fun it was to be there.
>
> **Patricia:** Walked there with a friend to have an excuse to go outside. Sunny and mild.

Day 22 of Isolation

Well, let's talk about the elephant in the room, shall we? Our governor put a "Stay Home, Stay Safe" order into effect several days ago. We turned on the TV for this briefing. We're letting Governor Inslee be the Bad Guy and break the news to the kids.

The reason he delayed this long is probably that Washingtonians thought "Shelter in Place" sounded too draconian, so he needed a few days to find something goofier than Cuomo's "New York State on Pause." I refer to it as "House Arrest."

Jeff pointed out that nothing has changed for us, because he was already working from home, and I was already reduced to drive-thru and grocery trips.

I counterpointed out that things have changed for our *children*, who had been playing outside with neighbor kids under strict rules. Lots of handwashing; no going inside people's houses; stay six feet away, etc. Now, they can only be with *us*. Which changes everything for us. He conceded my point.

If this will keep everyone's grandparents alive, I'm glad it's mandated, because I don't have the strength to comply of my own accord. I have followed restrictions thus far as best I can, albeit with heavy sarcasm, and I will do so with this one as well.

Later that day

Microwave door handle came off in my hand. In keeping with our quarantine tradition, we blame this on the Coronavirus. And, of course, I can't replace the part because the microwave is too old. And no one's doing new installations because of the virus. Crap-tastic.

Day 23 of Isolation

Why did the chicken cross the road? Because she was not subject to the stay-at-home order, and she could do whatever she wanted. Show-off.

WHO HASN'T FELT LIKE THIS LATELY?

Day 24 of Isolation

[Insert swear-word here.] Reboot. Try again in the morning.

Day 25 of Isolation

Sunday service in the living room this morning. Turkey, mashed potatoes and green beans for Sunday lunch. Because nothing says, "Pandemic in the Springtime" like a roast turkey feast... What can I say? I need the space in my freezer.

Day 26 of Isolation

Mary likes to do some different little thing each day for our morning walks. I've come to recognize this as her way of motivating herself to move through the day, which I can appreciate. (Hello, Diet Coke.) Today she completed our entire walk on a scooter, while wearing toy handcuffs. If *I* put her in handcuffs, I'd be arrested, but when *she* does it, it's adorable. Double standard strikes again.

Day 27 of Isolation

You know those digital billboards that cities use to post important, traffic-y things? Like roads under construction, accident ahead, and so on? Saw one today that read, "Don't flush wet wipes. Only flush TP." Guess you could call that a sign of the times...

APRIL

DISENCHANTED APRIL

I started sewing masks; I stopped cleaning. I became obsessed with fixing things that broke around the house. Probably because so much in my life became unfixable. And because everything kept breaking.

●●●●●●●●●●●●●●●●●●●●

Day 28 of Isolation

Twenty. Eight. Days. Add PMS and throw in some destructive meltdowns, and I cracked up. I came across a virtual choir presenting the old hymn, "It is Well with My Soul."[3] Do you remember the story of this song? The songwriter lost his young son, and the Great Chicago Fire crushed him financially. He sent his family ahead to Europe by a ship which sank in the mid-Atlantic, killing his 4 daughters. His wife telegraphed him: "Saved alone." He wrote the lyrics while his ship passed by their watery grave as he sailed to join his wife.

---

[3] See https://www.wsmv.com/video/virtual-choir-it-is-well-with-my-soul/

When the video popped up on my feed, I thought, "Well, yesterday was hard; today's not looking much better, but if he can *write* this, I can *sing* it."

I sat in my bedroom and belted it out along with the kind folks in the video.2

Mary, who was supposed to be doing her math, groused and grumped because of my singing.

"Too loud!" she said.

"Then go in another room," I said. "You don't have to be here."

I remind myself: Don't make their problem my problem. Her math is her problem.

Her school has to be finished before screen time; she must give fifteen minutes of solid effort for a rowdy brain-break with Dad. If she wants to wander around the house building with magnets (STEM!) or daubers (art!) to procrastinate — is that my problem? She's quiet. Since she's supposed to be doing math, she's avoiding us, so she's playing *independently*. The fact that she might run out of time today for screen time is *her* problem.

The fact that she might scream and yell about that is, admittedly, going to be a problem for me, but could happen regardless, so no loss.

Day 29 of Isolation

Fun with Middle-Schoolers: Damien blew through his screen time by 1:30 PM, so I investigated. I mean... kid had been up 5 hours — 3 of those taken up with class, shower, and meals, and a couple of hours' worth of schoolwork and chores. So where did he fit an hour of Madden? Simple: he was playing during his school Zoom calls. What the heck?

> **Me:** Are you kidding me?

> **Damien:** I was still paying attention.
>
> **Me:** I can't believe you're trying to argue this point. What would happen if you played Madden during class at school?
>
> **Damien:** They would take away my phone.
>
> **Me:** Funny — that's what happens at Online Learning, too!

Guess he thought I wouldn't work that out. Silly Rabbit...

Day 30 of Isolation

It has started to seem peculiar and even dangerous to see people in movies dining in restaurants or when I read about people, you know, *shaking hands* or boarding airplanes and such.

> **Chelsea:** A character in my book traveled to Mumbai and I don't know why she's being so reckless.
>
> **Crystal:** I have the same thoughts. Like, "oh, this is obviously from *before*."

Day 31 of Isolation

I'm fond of the number 31, a prime number which reminds me of ice cream. I'm also fond of the tall guy in this picture. He went through a lot this week, because I went through a lot, and I didn't contain my feelings well. I tried for the past two Saturdays to organize a family walk in place of our usual workout at LA Fitness, and both walks flopped. Due in large part to Mr. Grumpy Teen, I'm not gonna lie.

Here, Saturday #3, Jeff pulls off a miracle: sister rollerblading, siblings not bickering, brother not on phone, Dad having friendly chat with son, and Mom listening to loud music on headphones. Bravo, Jeffry!

Later, he washed and vacuumed my car, but afterward, he couldn't find his credit card. We all searched for several minutes, with increasing desperation. I rooted in the garbage can! We unearthed Mr. Visa in his right pocket, stuck to the front of his phone. Did I mention Jeff had a long week? Also, I'm lucky to have him.

P.S. Yes, he wore gloves to use the vacuum cleaner, and yes, I sanitized my hands after diving in the garbage can.

Day 32 of Isolation

I want to stop *trying*. I don't mean I'm suicidal or anything — just weary. Spring break has sprung, and my kids expect to do whatever they want this week. They'll share the depth of their displeasure when I give them the same ole chores, screen time limits, shelter in place requirements. Haven't attempted to explain "CDC mask recommendations" yet.

But I *totally*, 100% get where they are coming from, because I want to stop trying to:

- keep the house clean
- keep the kids doing their part
- keep food in stock
- feed the kids the right food
- consume the right amount of food
- feed the kids the right amount of the right food
- exercise
- entertain the kids
- educate the kids stay positive, calm, and patient
- stay on budget
- motivate a teenager
- answer 500 2nd grader requests a day with sweetness and light

I want to chow down on fast food, read books, sleep... I could try to find a middle ground. Not my best skill — I'm kind of an all-or-nothing gal, but maybe. Because if I find the middle ground, "sweetness and light" might be easier.

Day 33 of Isolation

The New Costco Experience wasn't as bad as I expected, though the whole thing gave off an 80s era Soviet Bloc vibe.

We arrived at 9:55 AM for 10 AM opening. The line was about halfway around the building, but everyone settled six feet apart, so they kept us moving right along. Movement stopped every so often, as staff only allowed new people in when previous customers left. Thirteen minutes later, Mary and I arrived at the door, and the queue monitor passed us a decontaminated cart.

NOTE: only 2 people could enter per membership card. Too bad it wasn't "1 person" — I could've sent Mary alone to buy all the things. I would've liked to witness that. The peer pressure to wear a mask was daunting, but I hadn't sorted those out yet, so I played dumb.

I homed in on the paper goods and scored paper towels and TP, albeit non-preferred Kirkland brand. (Too rich for my blood: We're bottom-of-the-barrel Marathon people. Now, my family's backsides will be spoiled.) Bought twenty-five pounds of flour. I hadn't done that since I was a teenager, helping shop for a family of five! But I keep using the flour in the pantry, and not seeing any at Fred Meyer, so needs must...

My nerves kicked up when I couldn't find peanut-butter stuffed pretzels, but the kindly staff member pointed me to the rear of the warehouse. I trudged back again to secure them. Whew. #covidcomfortfoods

Which was just as well, because the line-up for the cash registers was about 85% of the way to the back wall, and quite near the pretzels. Customers 6 feet apart. Progress was steady, because one line fed all registers, which saved me from trying to guess which register was the fastest.

Had I but known, I would've targeted the self-checkout from the start. Self-check had no waiting and occupied Mary with scanning and organizing all the things. Bonus: free hand-sanitizer at the register.

Showed our receipt to the exit door clerks through a plexiglass window, and we were on our way by 11 AM.

Proving, yet again, the mysterious tendency for Costco to require a full hour, no matter what I do. The line for carts was longer when I left, so best to shoot for early arrival.

Daze of Isolation

I'll bet that line was moving slower by then, since people like me were wandering about in search of peanut butter stuffed pretzels rather than yielding my airspace to the next person.

Grandma Patricia: Wonder what Mary would have bought?

Me: A playground.

Day 34 of Isolation

I found some N95 masks in our emergency supplies. [Thank you, Hurricane Katrina, for motivating me to keep emergency supplies.] Mary and I wore them to Fred Meyer today, and I completed my shopping with fogging glasses and sweaty cheeks. I rallied myself to sew some for us, because N95 masks are not washable. Now this is happening.

And sew it begins...

As per usual, every sewing project reminds me of why I don't sew anymore. At last, once I got the proper top-stitching thread, re-loaded the bobbin, and replaced the needle, I started to gain traction. Progress was slow: three hours for the first one I made, and an hour for the second, but I wrapped up three while everyone else enjoyed an episode of Star Trek Voyager. Because they loved me running the sewing machine during their show every bit as much as I loved when my mom did it. Heh, heh, heh.

Day 35 of Isolation

Mary, brandishing her Dum Dum sucker: "Mom, Damien said my sucker was un'ppealing, and I said it doesn't even *have* a peel!" [Self-satisfied grin]

Day 36 of Isolation

Okay. I just... Alright: I'll say it. I haven't cleaned my house since Day 14. I can maintain one, max two, areas of my life at once. This week, I made masks. This weekend will be yard work. Next week, eSchool starts up again. Gmail inbox: overflowing. Finances: unmonitored. Hope we still have money in checking. At some point, cleaning the house will rise to the head of the list again, but — what? It's not like we'll have *guests*.

One of my coping mechanisms is clearly denial, because I was reluctant to take the N95 masks out of the emergency kits we keep. Because, you know — I should be saving those for an *emergency*.

In other news, my parents and sister came by to pick up some fabric masks I made for them, and I realized I could now be considered essential travel. Wahoo — real people! Albeit 6 feet away, and we didn't hug, and I put the goods on a table and walked away, so they could retrieve them. It's surreal that this is starting to feel ordinary!

Folks ask me, with some trepidation, how I'm taking the fact that school is cancelled for the rest of the year. I'm chill, because I saw this coming, what with the Covid cases surging and all, so I freaked out a while ago. Now I've accepted my fate. Or I remain in denial because of spring break and sunbeams, and I gave myself the week off from being a grown-up. Most likely that last thing. Whatever.

Day 37 of Isolation

I started a little tradition in our house called "Fix-it Friday." We dropped everything we were doing Monday through Thursday and fixed broken bits around the house. Patching and mending wasn't a barrel of laughs, but perks include instant gratification, respite from eSchool, and a legit reason to postpone housecleaning. Thing is, as soon as I fix one thing, something else breaks. For example, you may recall our microwave door handle broke off. Last Friday, I glued that little guy back on, saving us $300+ installation. Yay! Thank you, friends who suggested gluing! Thank you, epoxy!

Then this week, the garbage disposal started leaking, attributable to the amateur installer. (Me.) So, in *some* ways, Fix-it Friday was very timely, because I needed to fix the disposal. I didn't care, because the idea of pulling that d*** thing off again was SOUL-CRUSHING, and I couldn't face it.

I thought about calling Fix-it Friday off because of Good Friday but let me not spiritualize my procrastination. Let's call it what it is: depositing head in sand, hoping things repair themselves.

By chance, Damien's phone wouldn't install new apps, and I got to the bottom of that, which made an honest woman out of me. Fix-it Friday: I fixed a phone. [mic drop]

Day 38 of Isolation

Jeff reached a milestone today: he broke my previous record for "Number of Times Around the Traffic Circle." I only went 'round twice before other cars came along and forced me to exit, but he clinched *four* revolutions. To Jeff's delight, the entire family was in the car, so his performance was witnessed and validated by the judges. Jeff also holds the household record for Highest Speed on a Bicycle, but I am still the Easter Egg Stuffer champion. Who says competition is unhealthy?

Day 39 of Isolation (Easter)

I made Resurrection Rolls for the first time. That was a lark. I read that brand name marshmallows work best, but the Kroger ones were 50¢ cheaper. I was not about to run out for replacements last night. So, I took my chances on Cheap Jesus. I had a bad moment when I peeked inside the oven (tomb) and saw marshmallow leaking on the pan. I guess the leaky bits must've been the Holy Spirit, because they came out fine. The moral of the story is that even Cheap Jesus can rise from the dead, and God loves tightwads as much as normal people.

We dressed up in our finest sweats, and I put my all into brunch since I roasted my turkey in March and was not up to a ham. I was barely up to brunch, to be honest. The kids' baskets were markedly less creative than usual, but I made up for that with massive quantities of candy, so they overlooked the monotony.

Day 40 of Isolation

We have reached 40 days and 40 nights, and I'm wondering if sending out a dove would work? Last week had several positive days, and I thought we were catching on, but those days turned out to be a side effect of no eSchool. This first day post-break was harsh reality. Many suggested I scale back, but the district reduced school to 90 minutes, three times per week, so the workload is not unreasonable. Writing one word of the assignment and breaking for lunch is unreasonable.

Also, our ice maker broke. Somebody must think Fix-it Friday is a dare.

Day 41 of Isolation

Damien's fortune cookie tonight read: Now is the time to book that trip you've always wanted to take. Bwah-ha-ha...

Day 42 of Isolation

More Fun with Middle-Schoolers. Wednesday is "math day" now for both kids, and I'm lucky if I survive. Damien's class is working on polynomials and binomials. By 1:15 PM:

> **Damien:** Mom? You want to try to do this algebra problem?
>
> **Me, no hesitation:** No.
>
> **Damien:** C'mon... I worked on this last one for an hour!
>
> **Me:** No. You spent at least 30 minutes of the last hour having lunch.

Surviving Pandemic Motherhood on Diet Coke and a Prayer

Damien: Okay. I exaggerated.

Me: Why don't you text your teacher?

Damien, with complete lack of irony: Because... I want to do it myself.

Me: Excellent! Please go ahead and do it yourself.

Kinda walked into that one, kid.

Day 43 of Isolation

I skipped my February Costco run, so when they ran out of TP, I was... concerned. By the time school shut down, my concern had grown. We had twenty rolls. I asked Jeff to guess how long he thought that would last, and he said ten days.

I thought that might be a little conservative. So, for one of Damien's first "math" assignments, I had him review the past year of Costco receipts and calculate how long he thought twenty rolls would last. Result: 42 days.

That seemed too optimistic, so I reviewed Damien's work and came up with my own estimate: one month.

And thus, the Ehlers PANDEMIC TP OFFICE POOL was on.

Jeff: March 13

Krista: April 1

Damien: April 14

I'm sure you guessed by now who won. (Me — why mention it if not to gloat?) In fact, we unwrapped the last roll *on* April 1. The victory was a thing of beauty. I won a bonus choice of take-out restaurant.

Sidebar: Several of my friends installed bidets, or the equivalent. I'm not doing that. I was a foreign-exchange student in Japan, and my homestay family had a bidet toilet which did not suit my fancy. Or shall I say, didn't suit my *fanny*.

Their bidet toilet seat came with a dryer as well. Like a hair dryer for your buns. Note that all the controls were in Japanese characters, most of which had not been covered on my vocabulary quizzes at school. All I knew was that one of them had to be "flush," because the tank was naked: no lever of any kind. I'll let you imagine how that all unfolded.

Day 44 of Isolation

This week's Fix-it Friday kicked my a**. I, possibly, bit off more than I could chew. Painting was involved, which I loathe: so messy! Plus, the one pair of jeans I sacrificed to become paint pants 16 years ago were... um... not as loose as they used to be. Here's what we accomplished:

- Repainted inside of microwave door with authentic [i.e., pricey] microwave cavity paint.
- Cleaned the vent grill above the microwave, which was gross with greasy kitchen dust.
- Fashioned a cleaning shiv out of a toothbrush to scrub between the slats in the grill.
- Epoxied the tabs on the vent, which broke years ago, but I just met Epoxy.
- Epoxied someone's rollerblade brake, snapped off by repeatedly kicking kitchen floor in a rage. [Kicker shall remain nameless, but only one of us owns rollerblades]
- Repainted the microwave door again, because I got impatient and shut the microwave before the paint cured. Oopsie.

- Replaced hinges on cabinets holding our garbage and recycle bins. Poor Jeff had been tightening them for months to no avail when we caught on that they were cracked.
- Degunked those cabinets. Ew.

At this point, I think I can pronounce our microwave refurbished.

Do you doubt that I could finish all of that in one day? While tutoring my daughter on poetry and half-note rhythms? And baking fresh bread? Well, you're quite right. In fact, Fix-it Friday ended at 2:11 PM Saturday.

Perhaps you wonder where Jeff is during Fix-it Friday. Well, he's making money to pay for all the things. Like $17 cans of paint and $7.59 hinges. I don't want his job, and he doesn't want mine, and that's how we roll.

BEFORE: Rusty door leaving exposed metal. Could cause arcing. Rust flaking off in food not wonderful, either

AFTER: Bright, shiny door; safe food.

Daze of Isolation

BEFORE: Cracked hinge crumbled in my hands. No wonder doors hanging catawampus.

AFTER: Upgraded to anti-slam hinges, though they've not met *my* kids, so we'll see about that.

> **Jerre:** OMG I hate those cupboard hinges!! We've got a folding lazy Susan door that's on its third hinge in 2 years. And every time I try and fix it the kids learn a new swear word.

Day 45 of Isolation

Every six week or so, we schedule family haircut day, and we were all lucky to have our "hairs" cut right before the Great Shutdown. Jeff and Damien may have been the last men in Washington to have trims. Possibly the last in America. Today is our day of reckoning: haircut day, but no hairs will be shorn. I offered to be their barber, but they both turned me down. Go figure. Mary and I will be fine regardless. We rock a style I like to call "Shaggy Chic".

> **Aimee:** I cut my husband's twice. We have clippers and I did okay on the fade.
>
> **Me:** I wonder how long they hold out. I should scare up some clippers, in case.

Surviving Pandemic Motherhood on Diet Coke and a Prayer

Jeff: No, thanks. I will go with the "Forest Gump" look if necessary.

Me: You say that now...

Day 46 of Isolation

We're home from our road trip, and I should be doing my physical therapy, but what I'd rather do is brag about how I tried and succeeded at rock stacking today in Anacortes. You could say I rocked it. [snicker]

This is definitely a thing, because I come across stacks like this all around. Am I supposed to stack as high as I can or use five to represent The Elements? Wait — don't tell me. I don't wanna work that hard.

I irritated Mary, because I used the rocks she collected, and evidently she had them organized the way she wanted, and I messed them up. After our forty-six days together, you've gathered that I *richly* deserve a child like this.

Only the pink one was "mine," so I had to find the rest on my own. That was a little challenging, because I did not want to budge from the rock upon which I sat. Not to worry — Washington beaches are rock rich environments.

Each road trip, the trick is to find destinations that are open and nearly deserted, such that we can remain 6 feet distant from others. Today, two places prohibited entry, but a landlocked schooner with a forest growing on deck was available, as was this beach-side bike trail. Abby, our labradoodle, is elated to join us on Covid Sunday drives; before Covid, she languished at home.

DOGGY ROAD TRIPPIN'.

Damien: Hey, Abby, you want a crab shell?

Abby: Crab shell! I'd *love* a crab shell! They're my *favorite*! What's a crab shell?

Damien: [Tosses crab shell away.]

Abby: Ohhhh, I get it. A crab shell is a frisbee! Yay! I *love* frisbees. They're my favorite...

A CAIRN. ALLEGEDLY.

Trevor: It's called a cairn.

Me: Figuring out a name in a foreign language was too much work.

Trevor: G o o g l e

Me: I was communing with n a t u r e ... Google woulda' killed the mood.

Trevor: And Facebook didn't kill the mood?

Me: No, it did not.

Patricia: This is why they make superglue. In my opinion.

Day 47 of Isolation

Sometimes, we sync up with the rhythms of Pandemia, and I'm upbeat about things... and then the paint chips off the microwave door I repainted three short days ago. Making me want to run screaming into the night. I don't, because: big girl pants need putting on and [clearly] the microwave needs more furbishing. But inside? Much weeping and gnashing of teeth. Blerg.

Day 48 of Isolation

The microwave was about to become dangerous, what with the poorly painted part flaking off to *bare metal* and everything. So, reluctantly, I took that bad boy apart *again*, sanded the corner and repainted.

Since I was already in a foul mood and crummy clothes, I decided to fix the leaky garbage disposal. Pretty sure I found the culprit. The 4-inch rubber gasket came out looking like a 12-inch earthworm that had been run over by a car and left in the rain.

Daze of Isolation

Had to dash to McLendon's for a fresh one of those. Went in my paint clothes. They're lucky I didn't go in my cheetah slippers. (See above: foul mood.) I was so happy I didn't have to wait in line to enter!

I was also happy that my day-glo orange sneakers matched my paint-splattered shirt, because I'm sure that took my look to a new level. Now, paint and silicone must finish curing so that I can test my handiwork. Please, Lord, let my work be handy.

In other news, Fix-it Friday is cancelled this week, because it happened on Tuesday. That is all.

Day 49 of Isolation

Some of my athletic tops must be shapewear, because they make me look svelte. And they're hard to peel off. In any case, I'm relieved that I have strong support, because one thing I haven't worn in 49 days is a bra, and that's unlikely to change anytime soon. Jus' tellin' it like it is.

> **Bonnie:** I don't want to talk about it...
>
> **Me:** Mum's the word.

Day 50 of Isolation

The fastest way to cause my daughter to come searching for me with an *urgent* question is to go to the bathroom. So invigorating when she's on a video call at the time and brings her Chromebook *with* her.

However, I cannot latch the bathroom door, because that's the fastest way to cause my dog to scratch and bark until I let her in. Mind you, if I leave the door ajar, the dog could not care less. My co-workers have something against privacy.

Day 51 of Isolation

As you recall, I called off Fix-it Friday earlier this week. By the time Friday rolled around, instead of relaxing, I replaced the dimmer switch in the dining room and reinforced the industrial grade door stop in Mary's room. Yes, that's the 4th door stop she'd overcome; yes, it was industrial grade and bolted to the floor; and yes, she still yanked it out like putty. What can I say? We have industrial grade kids.

But I digress. What is *wrong* with me? Why can't I take a break? Oh, I remember: teaching. I mean, I can't sit still and wait for a 2nd grader to find 10 alliterative adjectives. (See what I did there?) That's like watching paint dry.

On the other hand, taking a bath or a nap or reading or checking messages is pointless, because I field questions about assignments or tech problems or food approximately every seventy-eight seconds.

Therefore, I need a low-concentration task, and the short-term gratification of getting something *done* and being in *control* of something is... intoxicating. My children may talk back, but that flipping light switch (ha, ha — there I go again) turns on anytime I say so. No whining; no arguing; no rolled eyes; no slammed doors. Just light. Or dark. Or dim. Or whatever I want.

Day 52 of Isolation

My kitchen is like a science experiment these days, and not because I haven't cleaned, though I can understand why you'd think that with me. No — we are hosting a busy ant farm, marigold seedlings on the windowsill and my crowning glory, sourdough starter! Growing! Look: I made *pretzels* with it, all golden and chewy!

Daze of Isolation

This is such a dream come true for me. In high school, I babysat for a mom who made fantastic bread from a starter. She shared her recipe and her starter, and I made so much bread. Heavenly. By college, I could no longer keep up with the care and feeding, so I had to abandon the cause. Since then, I have tried and failed at least three times to make my own starter — I can't fathom why. I'm smart. But let's move on. This morning, I arrived downstairs to effort number four: bubbling and grown!

And now, I shall change my middle name to Ingalls.

Day 53 of Isolation

Our typical Sunday Drive was not up to our typical standards. Blah weather, blah location, blah children's attitudes. Attitudes stayed blah when we got home.

> **Me:** Mary, please take your shoes, socks, and shells out of the car.

Surviving Pandemic Motherhood on Diet Coke and a Prayer

Mary, snarky: I kno-oow. I'm commming.

Me: Not sure how I would've known that, because when I first asked you, all you said was, "I am Groot."

#toomuchGroot

Me: [collects garbage from around the house]

Damien, sullen: I'll do that. Not like I have anything *else* to do.

Me, brightly: Hey, thanks! The upstairs is done. [hands garbage bag.]

#guilttripfail

MASKS: SO MANY USES.

I started doing this daily journal based on my cousin Jeaneen's suggestion, and she knows a thing or two about hardships, so I went with it.

Posting each day has become like one of those prisoner movies where the hero scratches a hash mark on the wall behind his mattress to keep track of the days. Only I'm still shaving and bathing and such.

Daze of Isolation

The day this all started, a friend of a friend in China said they were on Day 53. I made up my mind that if she could endure fifty-three days, surely I could. Fifty-three days seemed like ages, yet here we are.

Committing to post every day turns out to be quite vulnerable! Before the virus, I didn't post things when I had a hard day. Now, I've outed myself: I'm not always funny. Here's to our ups, downs, and blahs: we've all got 'em.

> **Lisa:** I enjoy living vicariously through your family. Living alone sounds "nice" I'm sure in the midst of your chaos but it isn't. I'd much rather be surrounded by Mary and Damien. We all have our own journey through this unknown valley.

Day 54 of Isolation

Fifty. Four. Days. For reference, China didn't start relaxing limits until their seventy-sixth day.

Co-taught similes, metaphors, and personification with two actual teachers on-screen and me in-kitchen. Made sourdough crackers, Creamy Turkey and Wild Rice Soup, and some more bone broth. Son played Mancala with himself; he won. He said he'd finally found a worthy opponent. [Groan.] Two hours of meltdowns. [Sigh.] In essence, a normal day in the new normal.

The soup was tasty. The crackers were crispy. Weather was balmy. The similes and metaphors were decent. Son was funny and beginning to work on assignments when he gets them, not the day they come due. Watching Mary follow along with her PE was cute. I'll focus on that. And head out to rustle up some Diet Coke, also tasty.

Day 55 of Isolation

I was wearing my mask in Fred Meyer when I sneezed. Out of habit, I turned my head and sneezed into the crook of my elbow. I think I should get bonus points for superlative sneeze safety.

Day 56 of Isolation

Where we do prayer night, because: active kid. The one addition that would've made this photo perfect was if a certain curly-headed teen was along, but he was at Zoom youth group.

Day 57 of Isolation

Today, Jeff gave birth to a child. Not an actual child, but he did close a sizable deal at work which has been gestating nearly nine months. He works for a massive software company, and his clients are equally massive companies. As a result, my husband plows through an absurd amount of red tape on a daily basis.

In fact, he got another email this morning, questioning the details of this sale before finalizing. I teased, "Were they upset that the signatures were in blue ink, violating their strict Black Ink

Policy?" In any event, the t's and i's are all crossed and dotted, and he's happy, so I'm happy.

I've been trying to convince him to work from home, even after Governor Inslee releases us to go out and play again. As part of my campaign, I tell him that the secret of his recent successes is that he's not stuck in traffic six hours per week. I think I'm starting to wear him down. Got a little boost from Coronavirus. By the time this is over, he won't remember how to find his office.

MAY

MAY-BE NEXT MONTH

I gave up on fixing things mid-May: too exhausting and the things wouldn't stay fixed. I came to accept that the school was not going to take my kids back this spring, and I became concerned about next fall. Rightly so, as events unfolded.

• • • • • • • • • • • • • • • • • • • •

Day 58 of Isolation

Fix-it Friday was awesome today — nothing icky or painty. Made new tiebacks for Mary's curtains, glued spine back on old Bible, and mended a tear in one of Damien's tank tops. Which he got whilst climbing a chain link fence. Which his dad advised him not to climb. So, he deserved the following edition of Fun with Middle-Schoolers:

> **Me, hands shirt:** Here — I F'd up your shirt.
>
> **Damien, takes shirt:** Uh...??
>
> **Me:** See? [Shows him the neatly mended tear, which happens to be in the shape of an "F"...]
>
> **Damien:** Good one.

Day 59 of Isolation

I'm not eating because I'm hungry. I'm eating because my child's taken 43 minutes to read 4 short lines of an 8-line poem. #ADHD #eschool

Day 60 of Isolation

After its initial promise, my sourdough starter plateaued and I dreaded starting over, but the little blob blossomed again. So much that I had to refrigerate it. I had to switch to a larger jar and punch it down to avoid overflow whilst I slept!

Today, after days of sourdough pretzels, sourdough waffles, sourdough cinnamon raisin bread, sourdough crackers, and sourdough pizza, I completed my first loaf of SOURDOUGH BREAD! The moment we've all been waiting for. Mary is convinced I can make anything out of sourdough now, and she asked me to make Sourdough Crustos. (Tortilla chips smothered in cinnamon sugar).

I am the proud owner of a sourdough starter. My kitchen boasts natural yeast, instant yeast, and nutritional yeast. I'm a yeast-aholic.

Day 61 of Isolation

Today's elementary school outfit included a fluffy, bunny-ears headband, a sparkly princess dress, and golden Mardi Gras beads. Whatever works, man.

Day 62 of Isolation

How to turn Arts & Crafts into PE: Make a five-inch dream catcher with a twenty-five-foot length of cord. Let child pull the needle through. Repeat 100 times.

Daze of Isolation

Day 63 of Isolation

It was time for my 5 o'clock pilgrimage to pick up a soda, in which I blast my new favorite station (Hair Metal Hedonists). Def Leppard came on saying, "Do you wanna' get rocked?" I consulted with myself and found that yes, I did want to get rocked.

In preparation, I slid open the moon roof in my minivan, placed my sunglass clips over my glasses, turned up my seat heater and overall pretended I was younger and driving a riverside blue metallic Camaro. I convinced myself.

An old guy behind me at that stoplight was enjoying what could only be a confection from the nearby Dairy Queen. Turned out he was still behind me when I was turning left into a business park. The only businesses open in the park now are Starbucks and McDonald's. I'm not sure where he was planning to stop for his post-ice-cream snack, but I like the way he thinks.

Day 64 of Isolation

Damien's science teacher gave them an entertaining assignment in which they use their physical characteristics, combined with flipping a coin to simulate genetic randomness, to create their

Imaginary Child. The directions weren't clear on what was dominant and recessive and when they were to flip the coin.

> **Damien:** Mom, can I get some help with my Imaginary Child?
>
> **Me:** You mean, my Imaginary Grandchild?
>
> **Damien, with a slight eye-roll:** Yeah.
>
> **Me:** Sure. I must say, though, Grandparents aren't usually this involved in the making of their grandchildren...

Day 65 of Isolation

My friend gave me some chili pepper fabric, which I worked up into masks. Both kids asked for one, which tickled me. Damien wanted to flex his new mask, so he volunteered to run into Fred Meyer with me to grab bagged lettuce for tonight. Which brings us to our next installment of Fun with Middle-Schoolers...

> **Damien, shows bag:** Is this the one?
>
> **Me, notices some wilty bits:** Is that the best one they had?
>
> **Damien:** It's the *only* one they had.
>
> **Me:** Well, I guess that's the one for us. My kids will complain, but they'll survive.
>
> **Damien, deadpan:** You have kids?
>
> **Me, laughing:** I don't look old enough, right? The mask takes years off.

Day 66 of Isolation

I cried uncle in my lengthy battle with our microwave when the handle came off (again) in Mary's hand. That was the last straw:

we're getting a new one. Well-played, Magic Chef IV, but who will be laughing when you go to the dump? [Evil cackle]

Day 67 of Isolation (Mother's Day)

Jeff reminded me of that old country song, "Eighteen Wheels and a Dozen Roses", as he set off for the store this morning to buy my festive breakfast: eighteen eggs and a dozen donuts. He recorded my preferred donut flavors, which turned out to be futile, because all the donuts are prepackaged now, and you get what you get.

We each had two with breakfast, and one after lunch. Except Damien — he wasn't hungry, so he saved his for later. (Rather brave of him, since the box rode on the backseat next to Mary.)

Bribing the children worked well — they were agreeable today, for the most part, and even entertaining.

At breakfast:

> Mary: You remember Lily?
>
> Us: Nooo...
>
> Mary: The dog? The one who laid babies?
>
> Us: Lilu? (Aunt Brenna's dog, who had puppies.)
>
> Mary: Yeah, Lilu! It's like her Mother's Day!

On our drive into the mountains:

> Damien: If that volcano erupted, are we far enough away to be safe from the lava?
>
> Jeff: That's not a volcano, but no, we would be in trouble if it erupted.

Surviving Pandemic Motherhood on Diet Coke and a Prayer

Damien: I know what I would do if it did — I'd have my donut!

Me: Glad your priorities are in order.

Day 68 of Isolation

Yes, I did *blast* Twisted Sister to calm down from a disagreement with my teen. I let the music wash over me and felt the vibrations in my muscles and bones. And I did so in place of "giving him a piece of my mind," and I bounced back. Sometimes, I prevail over my mouth. Whatever it takes.

Day 69 of Isolation

I walk in this business park 5 days a week, and I have for years. I never came across this patch of irises before. It was like a peek-a-boo garden! I credit Mary, because while I take an identical path daily, my free-spirited cherub wants to explore and change paths every 7.2 minutes.

Day 70 of Isolation

Seventy days should be some kind of milestone, but I've noticed for a while now that it seems less like a "day of isolation," and more like "a day."

Of course, now that I've grown accustomed to the patterns of house arrest, going back to the regular pace of life will seem alien and invasive. You expect me to, like, shower and put clothes on? Clothes with zippers and buttons? Then drive somewhere to attend your thing? Through *traffic*? #irony

> **Gwyneth**: I heard 60% of women aren't wearing make-up or pants.
>
> **Me**: Only 60%?

Day 71 of Isolation

Mary was searching for something in the car, and I surmised that she might be looking for one of the many things she left on her seat before I loaded her bike in the car this morning.

> **Me**: I moved your things before I folded the seat down.
>
> **Mary, still casting about**: Did you find a rock?
>
> **Me, looking at car that hasn't been vacuumed in 7 road trips**: A rock?

Day 72 of Isolation

Surely you are on the edge of your seat, wondering what I fixed for Fix-it Friday, and with good reason! I changed the light bulb in our oven! Yes, that's right — the bulb lay dim and neglected since we moved in, but with all these yummy things we're baking, we need to illuminate the oven. As you can see, the light made a world of difference, almost miraculous.

Okay, you got me: the light *plus* three hours of cleaning made a world of difference. The working bulb showed me how badly I needed to clean inside. Something I also have not done since we moved here.

Day 73 of Isolation

Our day was busy scrawling "Happy Birthday!" on tiny post-it notes and hiding them for Jeff to discover. Not sure how long we'll be finding those around — Mary kept re-hiding them in new places.[4] We wrapped up by singing him the Red Robin song, and I hope we won't have to sing that to ourselves again on my birthday in November.[5]

---

[4] The one we hid on the inside of the shower rail was there for 9 or 10 weeks. Jeff hangs on to things.
[5] Skip ahead if the suspense is killing you: Day 257 (page 176)

Day 74 of Isolation

Puyallup Fair is famous for serving fresh scones, and I couldn't wait to try them when I first moved to Washington. I tried them at the first opportunity, only to find that they were plain, white triangles of dough. Where I'm from, we call those "biscuits." Today, I made my grandma's scone recipe for breakfast: golden brown, filled with yummy, chewy, crunchy things. I guess what I'm saying is, "That's not a [scone]. THIS is a [scone.]" [Insert Australian accent.]

Granni Anni's Scones

1 ½ cups Bisquick[6]

1 ½ cups granola

¼ cup raisins

¼ cup sugar

¼ cup nuts, chopped

2 beaten eggs, add enough milk to make ½ cup liquid

Mix dry ingredients, then add egg and milk mixture to dry ingredients to form a biscuit dough consistency. On well-floured

---

[6] I never have Bisquick on hand, so I usually make my own. Try: https://www.mybakingaddiction.com/homemade-bisquick/

surface, pat dough into circle. Cut into 6 pie-shaped pieces. Place on cookie sheet. Brush tops with beaten egg. Bake at 400°F for 15-30 minutes until golden brown.

> **Brad:** When we are at the fair I tell my wife, "I'm not paying $1.35 for a biscuit." As she gets one.

Day 75 of Isolation

I mounted our bikes on bike hangers in the garage, hung a few other things, and organized our ever-evolving collection of sporting goods, garden tools, and house parts. I would have postponed this to Fix-it Friday, but I'm calling off Fix-it Friday.

It was fun while it lasted but was too much pressure! I can't always remember what needs to be fixed, and I don't always have the energy to fix anything. So, I'm going back to my old "when the spirit moves me" fix-it schedule.

Or, could be I'm hormonal (Okay, definitely) and by Friday, I'll turn energetic and... fix-y. The suspense! What will happen on Friday? Nobody knows...

> **Sue:** I'm all for Fix-it February. We're past it? Oh. Rats.

Day 76 of Isolation

Guess what these are? My feet. In my son's shoes. Let's see how long it takes him to clue in. He chose shoes I like for once, and they happen to be my size. He won't be able to cram them back on at first because my feet are super narrow and his are not. Bwah-ha-ha-ha... #quarantinegames

Daze of Isolation

Day 77 of Isolation

Today, Mary and I had a guest on our morning travels. Yep: my sourdough had a baby! We took Baby Dough to its new home this morning, where I hope it will be well-behaved, not pee on the floor, and beget many homemade bread products. Do your mama proud, Baby Dough!

Is it weird to talk to my sourdough? And put it in a seat belt? It does contain active *living* organisms... Plus: cabin fever. Perhaps I should call it Wilson?

Day 78 of Isolation
Delivered 50 masks for homeless to Crafter's Against COVID-19. We prayed a blessing on the wearers. I am given to understand that sheltering at home is crummy when you don't have one.

Day 79 of Isolation
Thank goodness I fixed something on Monday, because today was more like Screw It Up Friday. I overlooked a step in the mask pattern I'm working on, which wouldn't have been significant, except I'm stitching seventeen at once. So, I spent movie night with a seam ripper. Mary went on a writing strike and took several hours to complete a twenty-minute assignment. I lost my sh*t with Jeff.

I mean, we're good now: seams re-sewn, apologies made, assignments turned in. But it was rough. Some days are hormonal. Some days, I don't even have that excuse.

> **Ellie:** So, it was a different kind of fix-it Friday.
>
> **Me:** Well put.

Day 80 of Isolation
The school informs us that Sexual Health/HIV education can't be effectively taught online, so they're punting to the parents. Can I tell him, "Don't have sex and you won't get HIV"? Can I have extra credit for the following episode of Fun with Middle-Schoolers?

We each have chores assigned for the duration of house arrest: Jeff, vacuum; Krista, meals; Damien, laundry; Mary, dishwasher. Which is how this awkward moment happened.

> **Damien, holding up a sexy nightie:** Mom, when did you wear this?

Daze of Isolation

Me, busted: Why do you need to know?

Damien, returning fire: Well... I didn't see you wear it.

Me, trying for casual: Huh. Go figure.

Aaaannnd... subject change. I mean, that was not the first time a nightie went through the wash; just the first time he noticed. Here's hoping he doesn't put two and two together.

P.S. I'll bet they take off points because I hid the post from my son. #notthatbrave

Day 81 of Isolation

Everything is divided into phases now: The state has re-opening phases; the school has re-opening phases. They're not the same phases. We have a phase-o-rama around here. My day developed in phases, too.

Phase 1: Extreme irritability, improved by worship service, but irritability returned. Family wished they could stay safe and healthy at someone *else's* home.

Phase 2: Ugly crying.

Phase 3: Sunshine, laughter, and hiking outside with family in masks, and among other masked families.

Phase 4: Back home to our nightly routine. Daughter resisted bath and reading, but still did them. Mom made masks and did P.T. Son shadow boxed in room. Dad presided over all, and to all a good night.

Day 82 of Isolation (Memorial Day)

I woke up mildly energetic this morning, and I planned several neat things in my head. Then, Mary woke up and spent twenty minutes telling me *her* ideas, rapid-fire, and I found myself run-down all of a sudden. It was raining. We already exercised (Saturday), and we already went for a drive (Sunday), and did I mention the deluge?

What a perfect day to go to the movie theater! Wait... what? Oh, yeah — Coronaclosure. I had been saving a coupon for $5 off Trolls World Tour streaming movie release for this type of occasion. So, we took the kids to Fred Meyer, where each of us chose a box of movie candy and a favorite drink.

After that, we went to McDonald's drive-thru for my favorite drink. We made a brief stop in the kitchen for a token healthy lunch product. After that: off to the couch, where three of us ate our entire box of candy watching TWT. Can you guess who had some left in their box?

Day 83 of Isolation

Here lies my first puzzle completed under quarantine. 48 pieces. I'm not an ambitious puzzler. Mary refused to help me put this together, until I got to the last piece. *Then* she swooped in and "finished it" for me. My inner Little Red Hen was seething...

Day 84 of Isolation

It's not that I don't know I'm overwrought. My role in most arguments over the past 10 days could be summarized with, "I'm tiiiiiiiired." [Whiny voice] But how do I become *untired*? I depended on school hours to complete tasks, so I could be a reasonable parent the rest of the day, so now what?

I thought I was getting by, until my son came in near day's end. He wanted to ask me if I'd heard about George Floyd and the whole thing made him so mad and what would I do if I was there, and he thinks he would fight those cops! Which made me proud but all kinds of terrified.

I botched the whole discussion because I couldn't handle my own feelings of powerlessness and tendency to disagree with rants regardless of point of view. Apologized. Took a bath. Stayed up too late reading my book.

Day 85 of Isolation

Every. Day. The. Same.

Day 86 of Isolation

Today my coworker wore pajamas and shin guards to work. Because school spirit day dress code was pajamas, and because she just located her missing shin guards, and in her mind, she morphed into Mia Hamm. I'm down with that.

Day 87 of Isolation

Yesterday was balmy and sunny, so naturally today began with thunder and lightning, nixing our usual walk. Seemed like a fitting time to crack open another puzzle. Which brings up that sticky topic of puzzle ethics. As one dumps out the pieces, does one separate the little clumps that came stuck together? A serendipity, or cheating? What to do, what to do...

Day 88 of Isolation

Fun fact about road trips during shut down: bathrooms are hard to come by. Fast food lobbies are all locked, municipal and park restrooms are locked, and many gas stations locked their public potties. Except 76 station in Issaquah, which has an adorable ladies' room.

Grocery stores are a safe bet, but you have to listen to your kids beg for goodies, which is almost not worth the indoor commode. That leaves "back to nature" if you drive farther than your collective bladders can handle.

Pack napkins. The public restroom at Stevens Pass today was so disgusting that I chose the woods rather than try to be seated, and my standards are not super high for such things. All things considered, I think I've exploited more bushes in the past 88 days than my entire camping and hiking career to date

JUNE

Things began to open back up in June, little by little. Our virus numbers were still rising, but more organizations were finding ways to work within the restrictions. We started picking up library books from the sidewalk and taking turns seeing animals at the zoo. Restaurants blocked off half their tables and opened their doors. As a bonus: June meant at least we could go outside.

●●●●●●●●●●●●●●●●●●●

Day 89 of Isolation

Another destructive meltdown over here. When that happens, we move all personnel involved to their bedroom, because we've made bedrooms a lot more child proof. So, I guess that makes my kitchen the Danger Zone. Which makes the front hallway the *Highway* to the Danger Zone...

Day 90 of Isolation

Washington's stay at home order expired, but whatever.... Our county hasn't met our numbers, so we're still grounded. Bigger cities nearby are on 5 PM curfews because of rioters, so they're like, double-grounded. Can you say, "Major Metropolitan Area"?

Many counties are in Phase 2 and have been for a while. They're being very polite, not saying neener-neener or anything, though some officials were clear that they don't want us Phase 1-ers to come visit.

My town is interesting, because our border straddles two counties. Snohomish County is applying to proceed to Phase 2; whereas

King County is not doing as well. They're asking for a variance to enter a modified Phase 1. By the time this is all said and done, everyone will know where the county line is. All that matters is that my house and my McDonald's are in Snohomish County. Phew.

Day 91 of Isolation

Early in my quarantine sourdoughing, I made the Perfect Whole Wheat Bread, which we will call "Loaf 1." Loaf 1 rose to lofty heights, did not taste like cardboard, and didn't require white flour (which is cheating). My only tiny complaint was the one side blew out and looked a little misshapen.

No problem. I scored the top before baking. Like I have dozens of times before to prevent uneven rising during baking. Loaf 2 emerged squatty, dry, dense and caved in like a swaybacked horse.

No problem. I added vital wheat gluten. Which I bought twice by mistake. Now I have enough to last me for the rest of my life, because Fred Meyer is not taking returns. Even so, Loaf 3: dense and swaybacked.

Fine. No wheat gluten, but I let the dough rise a little longer by not preheating oven until it rose to 1" above pan. Oops! I left the dough alone a little too long, but the top was a perfect dome... until I scored it. At which point it collapsed to swayback horse again. Loaf 4: Like a capital M that had a beat-down.

Humbled by serial failures, I gave up on scoring. I wasn't going to add wheat gluten, but I figured, "what the heck?" I let the dough rise to 1" above pan, preheated oven and baked. Loaf 5 was gorgeous. I didn't take a picture, because I don't need one — my bread was *identical* to the recipe photo.

Which I included below, so that you can attest that had I adhered to steps six thru eight as *written*, I would've had this beauty all along. Instead, I gave the steps the merest glance because of my many years of baking bread. Pride goeth before the bread falls.

https://www.kingarthurflour.com/recipes/whole-wheat-sourdough-bread-recipe

Day 92 of Isolation

As we approach our "stay home" orders lifting (soon-ish), I find myself wondering when I will stop Isolation posts. I didn't start posting when the Stay Home order launched; I started when the school shipped my kids home. Because if my kids can't go anywhere, I can't go anywhere. *That* could go all summer, and they're talking about "options" for the fall. So... hmm.

But in the meantime, the irony of all this makes me laugh a little. I mean, this is a struggle for each of us in various ways, but I can't help but think that we will reflect on 2020 as the year we had to:

... tend our own kids.

... cook all our own food.

... do all our own personal maintenance.

It's exhausting!

Day 93 of Isolation

The first step of deisolation: our county moved to Phase 2. I'm so excited! Now, to find out if the places we go can afford to open under the remaining requirements...

> **Stephanie:** What do you call the process you must go through after "Shelter in place" orders to restore the warmth you once held for your neighbors?
>
> **Me:** I dunno'.
>
> **Stephanie:** De-ice-olation.

Day 94 of Isolation

Picked up groceries at 11:45 AM. Finished putting away at 1:27 PM. However...

- chicken is de-boned, shredded, and in freezer.
- bones are in Crock-Pot for broth with fresh-picked herbs from my patio.
- ground turkey is separated into one-pound packs in freezer.
- cauliflower cut, blanched, and in freezer.
- spices put in jars.
- red peppers are sliced up for dipping in hummus.

This is why grocery shopping requires a nap, even when Fred Meyer does the actual shopping. And they left out the milk, so I still have to go back by Tuesday for the milk sale. Grr.

Day 95 of Isolation

We listen to comedians on our Sunday road trips, which keeps the kids from fighting and prevents the teenager from putting his headphones in, and a good time is had by all. Highly recommend this method. The trouble is that when we go into the mountains, we lose cell service, and I can't go on YouTube or Netflix to start the laughs rolling.

So, I dusted off my CD collection, which contained two comedy albums. The one I chose, Bill Engvall [Heeeere's your sign...] had a few curses and a few cringey bits I'd forgotten — not ideal when you're listening with littles. I turned to Jeff and said, "Sorry — it was either this or Bill Cosby." Still having trouble enjoying Cosby. Bill Engvall it is!

Day 96 of Isolation

In reading, the teacher had the kids read a book about race, in which the author discussed how we are the same under the skin, but each with our own story. The teacher charged each student to write their story. Such as where place of birth, parents' names, race...

Those aren't simple questions for an adoptee. To answer fully brings up questions for her, emotions for me, and could even make her a target of ridicule.

I mean, a common "story" for a foster kid who is adopted would sound something like: I was born on x date. The police took me away from my birthmother when I was [born, 3 months old, 3 years old, 13...] because my birthmother was addicted to drugs and couldn't care for me. I lived with [2, 3, 4, ...] foster families until I moved in with my mom and dad, and they adopted me. I don't know who my birthfather is. I'm not sure about my race: only what I can observe in the mirror.

On a random pandemic Monday, I did not have it in me to deal with all of that. If I had more warning? Sure. If Sunday wasn't a poop show of behavior? Possibly. Instead, we answered only what was asked — when and where she was born, she lives with Mom/Dad/Brother, she likes pizza and ice cream and rollerblading and art. And I pondered that she and we could choose how much and when we reveal her full "story," whereas families of color cannot. Sitting with the feels.

Day 97 of Isolation

I walked into Jeff's office around 10:30 AM yesterday and said, "I can't do this right now," and he covered my shift with the kids, while working. I left, drank copious amounts of Diet Coke, read Facebook, got the car washed and detailed, and tried to behave like a human again.

Today, I didn't even make it that far. Jeff said to me around 9:30 AM, "Why don't you go?" I left, attempted to reset myself, and managed to come back and finish the day pleasantly.

Around 5:00, I cut out for a breather and a soda. I passed by people gathered by the main intersection to protest racism. I asked Damien if he'd like to join that, he did, and we all joined in. Jeff and I were twice the age of the other protesters, and Mary was half their age, but was tiny bit we could do for equality.

Day 98 of Isolation

Mary wore out half a dozen watches and clocks for her room, but she has to wait until 7 AM to wake me. So, each morning, she sneaks semi-quietly into our room to check my watch to find out if it's late enough. I pretend to be asleep while I await the verdict.

This morning, she came in around 6 AM. She couldn't see to read the time, so she tiptoed into the master bath to use what little light was coming through our skylight. I laughed inside. Baby Girl, if it's too dark to read the clock, it's not 7 AM. I'm safe.

Day 99 of Isolation

Ethical dilemma. A spider built its web in the doorway of our bathroom shower. I take baths. Do I tell Jeff or let him discover it? Full disclosure: the spider is at eye level for me. So, about the height of Jeff's mouth. However, it is a dinky spider. Beneath notice. I'd guess one could swallow it without realizing, for example.

Later: Well, I was hoisted by my own petard. If I had told Jeff, he would have removed the spider immediately. Instead, the little guy is on walkabout. In the bathroom. Next door to the bedroom. Where we sleep. #karma

> Sue: I'm sorry. Fire is the only solution.

Day 100 of Isolation

I was expecting this to be a momentous day, and it was! I beat the family record of Most Times Around the Traffic Circle! This record was previously set by Jeff Ehlers on Day 38 (page 35). Today: Krista Ehlers, four for the win![7]

Day 101 of Isolation

I was giddy with excitement about going to Denny's tonight: the first time we've entered a sit-down restaurant in 3 months! I washed my hair and dressed in my very nicest athleisure wear. The adventure was... anticlimactic. Our favorite server and friend now works days, so she wasn't working. Mary spilled her water. Damien was bored, so he made unfunny jokes.

---

[7] Actually, I only *tied* Jeff's record: he made it four times around as well. I thought I beat him, though, and it's my book, so...

Mostly, though, our listlessness was because the new uber-hygienic practices were unnatural and (dare I say) unfriendly. The tables were bare of condiments. Low restaurant capacity limits made for lonely acoustics. The QR code refused to produce the menu, which we needed because Jeff's usual was no longer offered. Getting out was liberating. We'll go again. I just didn't realize how many gradations "the new normal" would have.

Day 102 of Isolation

You'll all be relieved to learn that the spider from Day 99 of Isolation (page 77) was apprehended. He was charged with trespassing and sentenced to life on our patio. He had a smooth transition, though he resisted having his portrait taken.

Sue: I'm glad you survived.

Me: Yes, well, you see what I had to deal with.

Sue: I would have had to move out until he was found.

Day 103 of Isolation

My watch face went blank three days ago, yet I keep strapping it on each morning. Like maybe it repaired itself on my bedside table in the night. I've had several of these watches and replacing the battery doesn't help. Of course, once I open the case, I won't have the right size battery anyway. Then I'll need to order batteries. Then I'll have ten, and can't my watch just work?

Do you ever find that you can take *real* problems in stride, but the tiniest things make you want to crumple in a ball and cry? Or shake your fist at fate? Yeah, me neither.

Day 104 of Isolation

Today was what I hope to be the first of many exciting adventures in *delivering* stuff. I was allowed to go the kids' schools at the appointed time for "Last names beginning with E" to give back their library books, course materials, and sports uniforms. All of which had been sitting in my house for a hundred days, begging to be mislaid or ruined. What a relief!

The public library called me to say I can give them back their books, too. Soon, I hope to drop off the stacks of batteries to recycle, clothes to donate, plastic forks, borrowed DVDs and more.

Of course, I was not the only one glad to offload items! The middle school gymnasium, above, was overrun by all the bagged belongings that the staff cleaned out of lockers for the kids. I'm not sure who had the worse job: the poor person who had to clean out teen boys' gym lockers or the teacher who stumbled on 3-month-old snacks fermenting in 2nd graders' desks. I hope they got hazard pay.

Day 105 of Isolation

Fred Meyer has been out of liquid hand soap for a month. At least. Woodinville Costco is out. Lynnwood Costco is out. So, this is what it has come to: DIY liquid soap.

Yes, we are able to use bar soap. Yes, those same stores have plenty of bar soap. However, I cannot face teaching my children how to rinse the dirt and hair and icky stuff off the soap and store the bar properly in a dish to prevent the bottom going mushy. I don't even own soap dishes anymore.

Lo and behold those teeny hotel bars of soap lying fallow can morph into soft soap! I have all the ingredients in my cabinet. I also have all I need to make liquid soap from scratch, i.e., sans hotel soap. Which is a little cool and a little weird.

Day 105 of Isolation (the rest of the story)

You will no doubt recall that my soap desperation forced me to make my own liquid soap, which was a rousing success. The very next day, I ran out of flour. The horror! My sourdough was hungry! I ground through the process of Fred Meyer Clicklist, involving several iterations of checking the sale flier, rebate app, coupons, fridge, and pantry. I clicked "Place Order" and optimistically drove down to retrieve my groceries, only to find that they were out of flour! The one thing I needed.

I awoke this morning with a mission: Get. Flour. I phoned Safeway from their parking lot; they had flour; I went in. Not only was flour in stock, but they also had *choices* of flour brands and sizes. I was filled with a sense of derring-do and stopped at the soap aisle. Behold: liquid hand soap! Several brands! I bought some — my handmade soap won't last forever. Please note that the Safeway stands across the street from my Fred Meyer. I will remember this, Safeway. I will remember this, Fred Meyer.

P.S. As I went to fill all the soap containers, I found that one child's bathroom sink had no soap dispenser at all and the dispenser in the other child's shower was mysteriously full. Um... Ew.

Day 106 of Isolation

My sweet girl is persistent. To the point of perseverating. To the point of wanting to run screaming into the night. As an example, let us consider banana oatmeal.

Surviving Pandemic Motherhood on Diet Coke and a Prayer

Months ago, I bought a variety pack that included banana oatmeal. Months. Possibly even a year ago. Nobody in the family liked the banana flavor, but I am militant about not wasting food. So, I let both kids to put a tiny amount of chocolate chips in the banana oatmeal if they would empty the box. Which they did, and I never bought that oatmeal again.

Scroll forward to present day, circa 6:20 AM, 40 minutes before she's allowed to come in:

> **Mary:** Will you make a special breakfast?
>
> **Me:** No.
>
> **Mary:** How about banana oatmeal?
>
> **Me, groaning:** I don't have banana oatmeal.
>
> **Mary:** You can make some.
>
> **Me:** But you don't like that flavor.
>
> **Mary:** If I don't like the taste, I can add chocolate chips.
>
> [Aha! The banana oatmeal is a vehicle for chocolate chips.]
>
> **Me, with forced cheeriness:** No. Make oatmeal you like, then slice bananas on top, like we do with cereal.
>
> **Mary:** I can't — Damien is hogging all the oatmeal I like. IT'S NOT FAIR!
>
> **Me:** He can have as much oatmeal as he wants. So can you. Oatmeal's healthy. Go for it.
>
> **Mary:** Nooo... He's eating the whole box. We're almost out!
>
> **Me:** We can put it on the list. I will always buy more oatmeal.

[Seriously: Quaker has a less sugar version that is only $1.50/box. Kids can make their own. What's not to love?]

Mary: No — he's taking it all. I'll show you! [Stomps off to kitchen.]

Mary, reappears with four full boxes of oatmeal: See? Look how much we have left!

Me: uh...

This is why I don't rise and shine.

Day 107 of Isolation

Last Day of School. I'm violently ambivalent about this. Part of me is *so* relieved that my days of forcing, bribing, cajoling, and otherwise turning myself inside out to entice my 2nd grader to do 2nd grade are O V E R . Part of me is filled with stark terror about what I'll do with the kids during this camp-free, contact-free, travel-free summer.

Both of them bore easily. [Thanks, ADHD.] Boredom is like a slow, painful death to them. When Damien gets bored, he picks fights. When Mary gets bored, she makes her own plans, but is upset if we won't/can't implement them. Right now. They're gonna eat me alive.

Day 108 of Isolation

Check out who we discovered sunning himself on some water pipes on our morning walk! Well, the sun is not shining. I guess he was clouding himself.

Me: Found two more further along on our path. Welcome to Snake Con!

Mark: It's mating season.

Me: Those sexy beasts!

Day 109 of Isolation (Father's Day)

We tried something new: church on a road trip!

Jeff got to pick our destination (Mt. Rainier). The day started with a rumpus between the kids and me, but after that it was filled with mountains and waterfalls. I stumbled upon the download feature of Amazon Prime, which allows us to listen to shows offline. So, we had our choice of comedians to entertain us even in the boonies.

Day 110 of Isolation

First day of summer vacation. Big fight with small child. Made agreements in which she made her own schedule of when she would do the "good for you" things (bath, chores, meals, reading) and when she would play. She agreed.

Day 111 of Isolation

Second day of summer vacation. Child melted down any time she had to do "good for you" things. She ripped up schedule *she* made and agreed to. I guess she only agreed in principle. Parents want to run away from home.

> **Nancy:** Are we purchasing school clothes or more alcohol in August? Asking for a friend.

Day 112 of Isolation

Washingtonians will be required to wear masks in public beginning Friday. People would be so much more willing to don masks if they came with matching capes. Capes for all!

Day 113 of Isolation

I found a new game. Mary — persevering Mary — has caught on that she sometimes gets little treats in Amazon boxes. So, whenever one shows up at our door, which happens often, she drives me nuts asking what's inside. Now, I let her open them straightaway, and she will soon learn how boring the contents are. Tomorrow: vacuum cleaner parts. Next week: nutritional yeast. It's entertaining. You should try it.

Day 114 of Isolation

I read many tips on how to use masks, but they are all about hygiene. What about operating with a piece of fabric over your breathing holes? Such as:
1. You can chew gum with your mask on, but do not blow bubbles. I do, but I live on the edge.

2. If you wear glasses, tuck the top of your mask under the lenses to prevent them fogging up. In fact, take them off — you'll see better without.
3. You do not have to put on make-up if you wear your mask. And best not to, or the inside of your mask is gonna be all Shroud of Turin.
4. Do not ignore a runny nose. Enough said.
5. On a similar note, process all crumbs and other food particles because your mask is not a place to store a snack for later.
6. Masks with wires will stay on your nose. Or perhaps I have a more sticky-outie nose...
7. Order of operations: first, glasses, then mask, then earbuds, then hat. Even if you do that, accept that it will all come off in one jumble.
8. Remember to take your mask off when you pull away from the drive-thru. I know you're excited about all the fries, but you appear afraid you'll catch Covid from your car.

Although perhaps you think your car will contract Covid from you. Like ours did.

Day 115 of Isolation

My parents were Boomers. I'm Gen X. Millennials come after me. I predict my kids will be referred to as Zoomers. You heard it here first.

> **Brian:** I think Mary is too young to be part of the Zoomer generation. They haven't named that one yet.
>
> **Me:** But she's the best Zoomer in the family.... She gives lessons!

Day 116 of Isolation

Krista's Domestic Tradecraft, quarantine edition: Always carry spare napkins in your pocket. This is for when you need to go potty au naturel, or for the odd runny nose. Runny nose + face mask = no bueno, as we've covered. If you come across a toilet with running water, but the toilet paper roll is naked, you can be all, like, "No problem! My last toilet was a tree...."

If you carry enough of them, you can even offer some to the next woman in line. She may demur, saying she thinks she'll wait for the next one. Then perhaps you could mention, "Girl, we're on the side of a mountain. I can guarantee you the 'next one' is an hour and a half away." Or you could stay quiet. I mean, you tried.

Day 118 of Isolation

Crap. I missed a day. Whatever. It's all a blur anyway.

JULY

July was the first full month of the Summer of No Camps. I became a zombie, but we also had our first time away from the kids, and they from us. The cases in our state spiked, likely owing to July 4 festivities, so our reopenings plateaued.

● ● ● ● ● ● ● ● ● ● ● ● ● ● ● ● ● ● ● ●

Day 119 of Isolation

I almost never clear out my email inbox at this point. Because I used to do that while the children were at school or camp. Forced myself to skip TV time tonight and catch up on the urgent messages. I keep a folder of "should read" emails — you know: the ones that will make me a fantastic parent...

- How to Structure Summer for Kids with ADHD
- How Much Screen Time is Too Much?
- Sensory Play at Dinner is Healthy for Kids
- 12 Ways to Help Your ADHD Child Focus Without Medication

...et cetera

48 of those messages were clamoring for my attention. Many of them are "newsletter style," which means something like 200+ individual articles to read. Study. Discover all the things I should be doing besides trying to survive.

Heck with that. I took sixty seconds to click through them and now there are four. #mobettah

Day 120 of Isolation

We all accept that we can't beat the children. It's illegal. And wrong. Especially with a meat mallet. But no one ever said anything about beating their bags of chips and Tic Tacs to smithereens because you are so. sick. of fighting. about. junk food. And I need a new meat mallet.

Day 11^2 of Isolation

Jeff instituted "Mommy Friday Afternoon Off." Probably because he found me huddled and zombie-like under a blanket on the recliner yesterday. Not exaggerating.

I took full advantage. I put in earplugs and jumped in the bubble bath. After that, a leisurely nap. I was so excited, making lazy plans, that I forgot to cash in on my traditional lunch of free fries and a McChicken. So, I had fries for an afternoon snack. Because: *free*.

Day 122 of Isolation (4th of July)

We were hunting for a patriotic film and decided to introduce the kids to Top Gun. Damien was into the characters right away — the cocky arrogance of Maverick really spoke to him. I think he took notes.

Mary was bored and was even willing to clean her room to earn screen time, so she could avoid watching. Then the pilots had their first training exercise. Mary decided she'd watch a little longer, because it might not be as boring as she thought. In fact, it was kind of like Power Rangers. High praise from her. And thus, another generation is in thrall.

Daze of Isolation

DOGGY MOVIE NIGHT.

Day 123 of Isolation

A day of improvisation. We went to the beach, a Washington beach. So, ice cold water and rocks.

Damien brought swim trunks and towel but didn't bother to tell anyone until we got there, at which point he blurted his plans out in front of Mary. Then she wanted to swim but had no suit. I insisted everyone pack water shoes, but Jeff forgot his. He didn't bring a suit, even though he never met a body of water he didn't want to swim in.

So: Jeff is wearing his jean shorts and my sparkly flip-flops. Damien is wearing his trunks. He will be sharing a hand towel with Dad to dry off. Mary is wearing her whole outfit and is soaked. She will use the beach towel Damien brought in some creative way for the 2-mile hike back.

Abby threw up — I imagine she couldn't deal with all the mechanizations. She promptly lay down in her mess, as shown in photo.

The dog bile is right under the fluffy doggie. I'm not planning to tell Jeff or the kids that. It'll be between you and me.

Day 124 of Isolation

Today I tried to find discounted patio chair cushions at Fred Meyer. I suspected the "pollen" that Jeff couldn't scrub off our existing cushions was actually "mildew." Upon arriving in the seasonal section, they were loading the shelves with school supplies. Which proves that Fred Meyer has the same hopes and dreams that we parents have...

P.S. Chair cushions were a bust. I waited too long, but in my defense, summer's barely started in Seattle. As any Washingtonian knows, our rainy season ends on July 5th.

Day 125 of Isolation

The Coronaversary. One score minus one year ago a new marriage was brought forth... Our friend is a nanny, and she is blessing us by taking care of the kids, so we can go on our annual trip to Salish Lodge. This is our first break from the kids in 125 days. And — let's be fair — their first break from *us* in 125 days. The freedom is so satisfying.

Daze of Isolation

We ate the food we wanted for lunch, I went to the bathroom alone, and we had uninterrupted conversation for nearly an hour! Coming attractions include a nap, meals made by other people with a side of more uninterrupted conversation, and dessert, and possibly a non-animated movie, a bubble bath, more sleeping... Living it up with my first husband. He was worth the wait.

Left, 7:22 PM: Our dessert, called Damn Fine Cherry Pie, because this was the hotel that starred in "Twin Peaks"
Right, 7:26 PM: Mission accomplished.

People: So, how long ya' been married?

Me: Bought-the-exact-same-anniversary-card long...

Day 126 of Isolation

Final moments of the Coronaversary. 25 short hours, if someone was counting. [I was. I was counting.] We didn't squeeze in all our grand lazy plans, but we were plenty lazy, so we're calling that a win.

Day 127 of Isolation

Our nation is plagued by a coin shortage. Apparently COVID-19 has a corrosive effect on money. Fortunately, this only affects young denominations. Your money is safe if it's over 25¢.

Day 128 of Isolation

Cow Day at Chick-fil-A is cancelled thanks to Coronavirus, ruining our long-standing, two-year tradition of dressing up as cows to bag a free sandwich and make Chick-fil-A almost affordable. The whole cancellation is weird, because I didn't even realize cows could catch COVID-19...

Daze of Isolation

> Marci: COW-vid 19

Day 129 of Isolation

Number one son has a penchant for what I affectionately refer to as "recreational arguing," in which he will often disagree vehemently for pleasure, with no attachment to the outcome. On our last two Saturday walks, we spotted a garter snake curled on some water pipes. Today....

> **Damien:** Hey! Let's bet on whether the snake will be out again this week. Mom, what do you think?
>
> **Me, contemplates wager:** Yes. [firmly, with conviction.]
>
> **Damien:** Since you said yes, I'll say no. [cavalierly — does not care about result.] Winner gets a bite of the other person's hashbrown.
>
> **Damien, checks for snake:** He's there! I knew it.
>
> **Me, laughing:** Why didn't you bet yes?
>
> **Damien:** Because *you* bet yes. [Duh...]
>
> **Me:** But... couldn't we all bet the same and everybody be right?
>
> **Damien:** [speechless. nonplussed.] No.
>
> **Me, to Jeff:** It's a live demo of ODD.
>
> **Damien:** I don't have ODD — I have ADHD.
>
> **Me:** You have both.
>
> **Jeff:** ODD is oppositional defiant disorder: a tendency to push back on everything.
>
> **Damien:** I don't do that.

Arguing about not being argumentative. That's my boy.

P.S. He didn't even order a hashbrown today, thus making it impossible for me to collect my winnings. Stinker.

> **Eric:** Wait, you have more than one son?
>
> **Me:** Nope. Just number one son and number one daughter. And number one husband and number one dog. I guess I can't count very high.
>
> **Eric:** You made it to 129.
>
> **Me:** You'd be amazed at how much effort that took.

Day 130 of Isolation

We boarded our first ferry in a long time and explored Kingston on foot. The map neglected to mention the steep slope we had to climb, but we reached the forest at last and hiked around a little.

Forests are some kinda voodoo magic for my kids. Five minutes prior, walking up the hill, they were all, "My legs hurt; I can't walk!" and "Stop touching me!" The moment we entered the trees, Damien headed up front to blaze the trail. Mary began her quest to collect all the things. Jeff and I took a breath. We would still be in our emerald refuge, but eventually the children insisted on having actual food.

> **Mary:** Mom, look! I found two ladybugs and they're stuck together.
>
> **Me:** Tell them to get a leaf.

Day 131 of Isolation

I needed a 69¢ bunch of cilantro to make supper but did not want to change clothes to go to Fred Meyer. I was still in my summer PJs: shortish shorts and a tank top. That wasn't so bad, but when I pulled up to the store, I realized I was also wearing my fuzzy cheetah slippers.

This gave me a little pause. I'm a stone's throw from the age where I no longer have any shame, but not quite there. Then I remembered that I would have a mask on the whole time! Nobody will recognize me. Problem solved.

> **Ken:** Oh Krista. What next? Curlers?
>
> **Me:** I'd have to buy some, but they *would* round out the effect.
>
> **Eric:** You just needed an excuse to wear slippers in public.
>
> **Me:** I had an excuse: it was after my nap.

Day 132 of Isolation

It's disturbing how often I pass abandoned underwear on the path during my morning walks.

> **Author's Note:** There were about 70 comments of "ew" to this, so I presume no one wants to see a photo of same. Though I did not refer to gender, people universally (and correctly) assumed that they were men's underwear. Just sayin'.

Day 133 of Isolation

I have a degree in computer science, eight years in tech support, and several years as a freelance web developer. Even with all that, having both students learning online and Jeff working from home full time has tested my patience and skills to the limit.

My daughter, however, has a controlling streak a mile wide and some technical chops of her own. Consequently, she is quite ambivalent about getting help. Today her drone was giving her fits.

Surviving Pandemic Motherhood on Diet Coke and a Prayer

All four propellers are labeled: two marked A, and two marked B, and the A's and B's must be alternated, or the drone won't fly.

> **Mary:** My drone won't fly. Can you help?
>
> **Me:** [Takes drone, squints and squirms to make out the infinitesimal A or B on each propeller.]
>
> **Mary:** [grabs for drone] I can do it!
>
> **Me:** Then why did you ask me for help?

Gaaaaaahhhhhh!

Day 134 of Isolation

The watch on the left is the one whose battery died on Day 100 (page 77), which I took to the jeweler, who was awesome. He replaced the battery, but neither of us could adjust the time. So... the date January 27 in Left Watch World.

The watch on the right is the one I ordered from eBay to replace the un-adjustable one. Right Watch arrived on Day 115 and died last night. There comes a time when you have to admit defeat and buy a new frickin' watch

Day 135 of Isolation

This old guy kept calling my cell phone in error.

RING [from Private Number]

Me: Hello.

Old Guy: Huh? I can't hear you...

RING [from Private Number]

Me: Hello?

OG: What? Can't hear a thing.

Me: Who is this?

OG: Barry!

RING [from Private Number]

Me: Hello? Who are you trying to reach?

OG: Kim!

Me: This is Krista. There's no one by that name here. I think you have the wrong number.

OG: Oh. Sorry!

RING [Next day, Private Number]

Me: Hi. It's still Krista.

OG: Kim?

Surviving Pandemic Motherhood on Diet Coke and a Prayer

Me: Nope, no Kim here. What number are you dialing?

OG: Um... 1-800-THE-VOICE.

Oh. My. Word. His name isn't *Barry*. He is dialing The Voice to vote for Kim *Cherry*. Who was eliminated a year ago. I swear, next time Imma' tell him we got his vote for Kim, thanks for calling. If he keeps trying, I will tell him Kim won, and she's grateful for his support.

Day 136 of Isolation

This week, Mary and I went to Costco, and they had our brand of TP for the first time since outbreak — Marathon. For reference, this is the cheapest toilet paper they sell for home use. The brand packaged in those wrappers that sound super loud when you need a new roll at 3:27 AM.

It's comforting to have this back in my cabinet: Everything is so chaotic and surreal, but at least something is back to the way it was. We buy this cheapie TP because I can't make my family to realize that you don't need as much of the thick and luxurious brand. I guess what I'm saying is: nothing but the worst for my babies' bums. And noses. Because Kleenex is right out.

Later that day

My dead watches, cuddling on my nightstand, as though I'm hoping they'll mate in the night and birth a single working watch.

Daze of Isolation

IT COULD HAPPEN...

Day 137 of Isolation

I reluctantly parted with $160 for the annual Woodland Park Zoo membership. Although we paid a steep price, after only two visits, I will have saved $5. I figure we could swing two trips in a year — we used to go all the time. *Five* whole dollars... I'm unclear myself if I'm being sarcastic or I'm that cheap.

Jeff found out why I stress myself out packing snacks for our adventures, because I thought I could avoid packing any this time. Not sure what I was thinking. Mary reminded us about her severe and unrecoverable hunger after nearly every exhibit. Right up until the point when she fell asleep in the car on the way home.

Jeff and I weren't much better. On previous trips, we always parked in the same lot, rested at the same restroom, viewed the exhibits in the same order, had lunch by the penguins, and wrapped up at the Family Farm. We stopped at all the climby places like African Village, Zoomasium, and Bugs World. For obvious reasons. You know — to combat hunger strikes. Except all those exhibits are roped off due to Covid.

Having to park in the Flamingo Lot, but wishing we'd parked in the Otter Lot, and then begin in the middle... We were disoriented from penguins to piglets.

Day 138 of Isolation

On my walk this morning, I wasn't paying attention, and I got sprayed full in the face by a maladjusted sprinkler head. Alright, I was walking and texting on my phone, if you must know. Ironically, Damien pointed out two days ago how that sprinkler was watering the sidewalk. He'd laugh his butt off if he'd seen me, so none of y'all rat me out, now, hear?

P.S. You can spot the culprit, below. As I was capturing this photographic evidence, another sprinkler head got me from behind. They're gunning for me.

Jeff: You forgot to tag Damien on this post...

Me: I didn't forget. If he can't find it on his own, he misses his chance... #toughlove

Daze of Isolation

I saw a mangled sprinkler head lying on the sidewalk across the street from those sprinklers a few days later. Humans are fighting back.

Day 139 of Isolation

Jeff is so patient with my Diet Coke addiction, but even he gets tired of frequent stops for $1 sodas. I can't trust myself to keep bottles or cans in the house and, besides: McDonald's fountain drinks are the best. From time to time, he gently points out that they're cheaper and closer at 7-Eleven. McDonald's gave him a boost for his case this week, as their soda machine broke down several days ago. I couldn't avoid the irony when I spied the crew pour my soda from a 2-liter bottle. I saw those moments ago on sale at Fred Meyer for 99¢.

Defeated, I stopped at 7-Eleven and gloved up to pour my Big Gulp.

> **Jeff:** Could you tell the difference between 7-Eleven and McDonald's soda?
>
> **Me:** Well, yeah. I had to park my car, exit my comfortable car, hike to the back of the store, dispense my own drink...
>
> **Jeff:** [rolls eyes]
>
> **Me:** ...and then, I had to hike all the way back to my car to drive home.

Alas, McDonald's is still out of Diet Coke, so I even downloaded the 7-Eleven app. They're offering me my first seven sodas free. Clearly, they long for my addiction business.

P.S. For anyone who scoffs at me for balking at walk-in vs drive-thru, I'll let you take my children with you next time you want to "dash in" and grab a soda... You will not be thanking Heaven for 7-Eleven. Of course, if you scoff at my dependence on Diet Coke, well... Go ahead. I deserve that scoffage.

Day 140 of Isolation

The clock is ticking. Already 2:14 PM and I have no idea what I'm gonna feed these people tonight. What I do have is an accurate grocery list to submit for pick up... tomorrow. I'll print that out, and they can nibble the pictures. Roughage.

Later that day

I'm rallying, but I do not have the time to drive to McDonald's for Diet Coke. Nor the energy to traipse all the way into 7-Eleven. Gonna have to bust out the Cooking Tiara. Of course I'm not kidding! I would never kid about tiaras.

Day 141 of Isolation

Some of my friends are squeamish when hearing about lady things. I won't name names, but you know who you are: best turn the page. Jeff and I had an interesting June as my cycle was a month

Daze of Isolation

late. I'd never been more than a day late in my life except for three times, all resulting in pregnancies and miscarriages.

We kept looking at each other all month, wondering if we were about to experience an incredible miracle, for which we felt stark terror. Two is all we can manage! I commenced eating for two. Y'know: to get a jump on the stress I might be about to encounter. After all the suspense, my body... got back to normal, so I guess we're looking at perimenopause. Because that's what this quarantine needs: hot flashes and [more] irritability. Now I'm off to work on losing my not-baby weight.

Day 142 of Isolation

You will be curious whether my sourdough is still a going concern. I can report with pride and not a little surprise that my sourdough is alive! Every time a pan of bread rises is a personal victory. Or pretzels, or hamburger buns, or rolls... The yeast is so magical, floating in from air to make all the things. It's like free bread. It's like making bread outta' nothing at all.[8]

Late last Saturday night, I fed my starter, in order to pack fresh bread for a picnic lunch at the zoo. I rose, bleary-eyed, at 6 AM Sunday to mix the dough. By noon, the dough had not risen, forcing my family to eat leftovers for lunch. [Gasp.] Though a disappointment to all, I did learn two valuable lessons.

Number 1: My sourdough is perfectly willing to take a nap in the refrigerator, come out later, rise to its full stature, and make a very lovely midnight snack.

---

[8] It's never a bad day when you can work in an Air Supply reference.

Surviving Pandemic Motherhood on Diet Coke and a Prayer

Number 2: My sourdough, like myself, is not a morning person.

Day 143 of Isolation

Exodus tells us that God made manna fall from Heaven to feed the hungry Israelites, but scholars disagree about what manna was. Resin? Lichen? A form of Hoarfrost? Jeff solved that mystery forever in tonight's Early Reader's Bible reading:

Beers, V. G. (1995) *The Early Readers' Bible*. Zonderkidz.

"I want something to eat," a little boy said.

"We want something to eat, too," said his mother. "But there is no food."

"God will give you [Chicken McNuggets]," said Moses.

See illustration. The answer is so obvious. Why didn't the Scholars check the Early Reader's Bible?

Day 144 of Isolation

Usually, we just take a nature walk and call it a hike, but today's choice, Wallace Falls, was a legit hike. Reminded me of when Jeff used to lead activities for our church group. He would organize a half dozen or so training hikes, and then we'd climb Mt. St. Helens on Labor Day. He did that for 10 years. (Point of information: I reached the summit once. To show I could.) In between those, he was a distance runner/marathoner and later, triathlete.

In those days, he scampered up the mountains, ahead or way ahead of the group, and greeted us cheerfully at the summit. These days, he brings up the rear with me. Not because of age: because he wants to make sure kids and/or the dog aren't torturing me with themselves. I have come a long way in my fitness, so the hike was taxing, but doable. Sure, I was drenched in sweat, but the temp was over 80° and plus: menopause.

As we hiked, a question sprung to mind.

> **Me:** Hey! On all those hikes... were any of those a challenge for you?
>
> **Jeff:** No. Well, except for that one...
>
> **Me:** When you got dropped by that guy who turned out to be a meter reader in his day job?
>
> **Jeff:** Yeah. [pause] And the time your brother went.
>
> **Me:** [Basks in the reflected glory of being the sister of someone who beat Jeff to the top of Mt. St. Helens.]

Day 145 of Isolation

My last sourdough loaf was thick and sticky and baked into a hard, tasteless brick. Think I forgot to put in oil. Or the dough had

PMS. Today's loaf was back to its normal fluffy-yummy self. Can't win 'em all. Brick in compost bin. Nobody saw that.

Day 146 of Isolation

Work day at church! We needed to move all the seating into the hall to prep for new carpet, which meant unscrewing over 2500 bolts. I brought the muscle (Damien) and the ladybugs (Mary) and the slightly skilled labor (me). Though when I got the ratchet stuck under the *first* chair I worked on, they demoted me to unskilled. Fair enough.

Mary went in with a ladybug in the bug jar she got in her Vacation Bible School in a Box; she went home with an empty bug jar. Oops. If you find the ladybug, don't call me: bug earned its freedom. If you find a pale yellow, Mary-sized, fabric mask, though, send that my way. (Why did she take it off in the first place!?! Grrr.)

Damien comported himself very well in the heavy lifting, so at least one of the team lived up to expectations.

Day 147 of Isolation

I forgot to mention how thrilled my kids were to wake up early and go to the work day. They both got up and ready to go so fast that we arrived 30 minutes before the start. Shows how not-thrilling our other days are.

Since we arrived well before the others, they let me operate the temperature-taking-gun. I was heady with the power. I kept saying, "None shall pass." They let me keep it through prayer time, but then I had to relinquish it. I bet they gave me the ratcheting socket wrench to lure me away from the ray-gun thermometer. Hey, shiny!

Day 148 of Isolation

Mary woke us up this morning pleading to set the suitcase out, so she can begin packing for our mini-vacation that starts in four days. Jeff kept trying to say it was too soon to start packing, but I stayed shut. I started days ago.

- Yesterday was meal-planning day.
- Today was cooking day.
- Tomorrow will be grocery day, plus more cooking.
- Saturday will be packing clothes and non-perishable food, haircuts, wash car...and lose my mind, because I will run out of time to finish all the things.

It's how I do trip prep. Forewarned is forearmed. Not sure who should be armed. In fact, armaments would be a dreadful idea at this point. Who thought that up?

Day 149 of Isolation

> **People**: My, what a fine bike helmet you're wearing little girl.
>
> **Child**: Yes, I have to borrow my mom's fancy, expensive helmet because I can't find my helmet, and she's still too mad to fork over the money for a new one...

Again.

Between what gets permanently lost and what gets broken beyond repair, we rebuy our household about every 347 days.

Don't even remind me about time spent finding and repairing. Jeff says this is some kind of karmic payback for the number of things he lost when he was a child. To that I say, why can't karma forgive and forget?

AUGUST

ANGST-US

We had our first family vacation since Covid. Escaping our same old four walls was fantastic, though cleaning our own hotel rooms was a drag. This is why I don't do VRBO.

●●●●●●●●●●●●●●●●●●●●●●

Day 150 of Isolation

Saturday was devoted to creating this masterpiece of human engineering: all the Ehlers packed in the car, headed to Skamania Lodge for our first Covid-Vacay.

- Four shorn heads
- Food for ten meals and boundless snacks

- Five days of Vacation Bible School (this was not my handiwork: our children's pastor wrapped all the goodies up in a tidy package!)
- Miscellaneous clothes, flip-flops, sunscreen, a football, dolls, and dog food.

I'll be honest: it was rough. Everybody snapped at everybody. I came unglued around 5 PM and didn't become glued again until after the kids went to bed. (Go figure.) I hate how this is always a part of my family's vacation experience. I keep trying. This morning was better, though a little rocky. Do our smiles seem strained? Breathing in, breathing out...

Day 151 of Isolation
In which Jeff and Krista find out they're not "in love"...

> **Damien:** Fun Fact — if you're next to someone you love and hold hands, your heart rates sync up.
>
> **Jeff:** Impossible. Mom's resting heart rate is 71; mine is 42. If she synced up with me, I'd put her in a coma.
>
> **Me, indignant:** My resting heart rate is under 60... Besides, the point is that simply being *next* to me would raise your heart rate.
>
> **Jeff:** [rolls eyes]

Then, with the unspoken communication which comes with 19 years of marriage, we joined hands and activated our heart rate monitors.

> **Jeff:** 56.
>
> **Me:** 64. Wait! Mine's going down... 60.... 58.... 55... 54!

Daze of Isolation

Jeff: [measures his again] 44.

So, the results were inconclusive. I maintain that our heart rates were, in fact, in the process of syncing up, we just needed to wait longer. Because, as we all know, you can't hurry love.

Day 152 of Isolation

Started our Vacation-Bible-School-in-a-Box curriculum today in the hotel lobby. Mary enjoyed herself in spite of me, and I was reminded why I am not a children's pastor. For one thing: *so* little patience. For another: I *cannot* make slime. I now own a half gallon of raw material, and we are going to have slime by the end of this frickin' summer!

> **Linaya:** We made our sundials and it's not lining up. I've come to the conclusion that I'm not at fault here. Clearly, the sun is not working!
>
> **Me:** Your logic is flawless. Funny, because our hotel has a giant sundial, which Damien tried to read. He said, "This is amazing! Mom, is it 8:50?" I said, "No, 9:50." It's disturbing how long it took us to realize that sun dials don't account for daylight saving time!

Day 153 of Isolation

The older kid snapped at the younger one in the night for sleep-talking and, later, for using her flashlight to go to the bathroom. He says he was asleep. If true, that means they even bicker in their sleep. I'm starting to wonder about our sanity for taking four people who bickered in 2200 square feet and squeezing them into a 200 square foot room. What can I say — we like a challenge?

> **Fran:** Sanity? You have young children, and you expect sanity as well?

Ellie: Every. Single. Trip. Ugh

Ric: 'Question for my essential oil friends. Which oil calms housebound family members down? Chloroform? It's chloroform, isn't it?'

@ THE POOL, COVID-STYLE

Day 154 of Isolation

You can tell by now that I use humor to cope with trials, and my fondest wish is to pass that on to my kids. (The humor; not the trials. I pass those on by accident.) I think they are well on their way...

> **Jeff, pointing to a partly submerged tree trunk (in photo):** Cool! It's like a sunken ship.
>
> **Me, having recently visited the zoo:** I think it's like a hippopotamus.
>
> **Jeff:** Let's ask Mary.
>
> **Mary:** It's a ship.

Daze of Isolation

As we hiked a little further along, we passed by a decrepit wooden bench which had collapsed on its side.

> **Jeff:** I wonder who knocked over that bench?
>
> **Mary, deadpan:** It was the hippopotamus.

Day 156 of Isolation
You'd I think I would be ecstatic that our health club is reopening on Monday, but...

- The pool is not open yet, so Jeff can't go.
- The childcare is not operating yet, so I can't go.
- Damien's membership requires a parent go with him, so he can't go.

I'm not unhappy that they are reopening, because an open gym is one step closer to something that would be useful to us. Other people will surely go, but this is why we're still "in isolation".

Day 157 of Isolation

We got word Thursday that the district is shutting off access to i-Ready, which is what we're using to keep Mary up to speed on math and reading. They need to prep for the new school year, and I sympathize; but I fought tooth and nail to coerce Mary into the habit of fifteen minutes of academics per day: I'll be darned if I'm giving that up!

I told Mary that I thought she would like "time off" from i-Ready, so we're going to start "getting ready for 3rd grade" by switching to Typing Club, where she can learn to type fast "like Mom and Dad," to make her 3rd grade work easier. Every statement 100% true, only a little bitty white lie of omission...

> **Me:** Grandma *Sherry* types very fast.
>
> **Mary:** Oh, I want *her* to teach me!
>
> **Me:** What a great idea!

Day 158 of Isolation

Since we can't dine in at most restaurants, we pick up takeout and try to find somewhere pleasant to sit with our food, like a scenic overlook or a park picnic bench. Because I'm cheap, we stop by McDonald's to grab $1 sodas on the way to the pleasant place. As we were leaving McDonald's the other night, I turned to Jeff.

> **Me:** Thank you for being so patient with my foibles.
>
> **Jeff, graciously:** We all have our foibles.
>
> **Me:** Yes. I'm guessing I have more foibles than other people. In fact, I'm exceeding expectations!
>
> **Jeff:** [blank expression]

Daze of Isolation

Me: I'm above average!

Jeff: [Eyes on continuous roll.]

Me, perky: I'm *winning* at foibles!

Later that night, as I was rearranging the garbage to fit my soda cup:

Jeff, sardonically: Seeing if you can stuff one more thing in before I have to take it out?

Me, guileless: Of course. [Washes hands.]

Thereby revealing another of my foibles, in which I believe that the person who can't shove any more garbage into the can is the one who must empty the bin. Which is why I always build an orderly tower of soda cups in the corner of our kitchen garbage can, because slipping one more on the stack takes up almost no space. It's *efficient*.

Day 159 of Isolation

I forgot what I was gonna say. I bet it was something awesome. Maybe I'll remember if I go stand for a while in front of the fridge with the door open. Always seems to work for my kids.

Day 160 of Isolation

I still smile at people when I'm wearing a mask, though my mouth is hidden. My eyes turn squinty when I smile, which hopefully they interpret as a smile and not a scowl. Squinting is the new smile.

Day 161 of Isolation

Our first expedition to IKEA since the plague. We arrived a half hour before the doors opened, but over fifty shoppers were already wrapped around the retractable belt barriers.

To prevent Mary from pestering, "Are we almost there?" all the way, I told her that we start at exit 26, and IKEA is at exit 2; each number equals a mile, and each mile takes about one minute. Unintended consequence: non-stop updates on our progress...

What's the exit? 24. Okay. Next exit is 23. 23 A or B? Here's 22. 20! Next will be ninnneteeeen.... Oh, 18. Okay. Sevennnnnteen... Here comes 14. Where was 15?

We had a brief intermission between 10 and 7 while she discussed at length the thorn she found in her shoe, which she put back into the shoe, so she could show Grandma. Then we were back to the play by play. She doesn't so much "talk" as "narrate."

But she never asked, "Are we almost there?"

And she's building valuable navigation skills.

Right?

Day 162 of Isolation

Today was a low-laughter, irritating, grumpy-Mommy day and deserves to be skipped. So moved.

> **Andy:** I second the motion. Since there is no dissent, motion carries, so be it written, with hugs all around.
>
> **Me:** Always handy to have a friend familiar with Robert's Rules of Order.

Day 163 of Isolation

Much better than yesterday — glad we skipped it.

Daze of Isolation

I just found out that Value Village reopened. Why didn't they tell me sooner? I've been holding off as long as I could, but both kids are bursting out of their current sized clothes, so I almost had to pay *full retail* for clothing! That was a close one.

I started with the Woodinville location; then I tried to go to Totem Lake, only to find a dark and empty building. So, we continued on to try the Redmond Value Village for the first time. Scored several items for kitchen, kids, and me.

Damien is now shopping in the Men's section, so that's weird. He walked up to me with three pairs of jeans, including one that was fashionably ripped. I was scheming how to tell Jeff, who can't stand paying money for jeans with holes in them. They were too tight. (Phew.)

In other news, Mary made her first scrunchie on her new sewing machine, and put up her hair all by herself, too. Perhaps she will be into ponytails now — they turn her into a Disney princess: all deep brown eyes and pixie face.

Later for movie night, we introduced Mission Impossible. Though I'd seen the first one before, I still had trouble tracking all the players. So, a typical Mission Impossible viewing experience.

Now, kids are in bed, so hot cocoa, Salted Caramel Crunch yogurt, and three Hershey's Special Dark Chocolate Kisses. Okay, five. Okay, maybe the rest of the bag. Whatever.

Day 164 of Isolation

BREAKING NEWS:[9] On our walk today, a massive tree branch cracked off its trunk and crashed to the ground behind me. So close

---

[9] Pun completely intended.

behind me, in fact, that I hardly knew whether to turn and gape or scramble out of the way! I can only tell *you*, Gentle Reader, because I couldn't mention what happened to Mary, who missed the whole thing. She's rather worried a tree will fall on us any blustery day. Trees falling apart on a sunny, windless day would make her head explode.

Here's something uncanny. The very next day, we drove past in the car, and saw that another limb had fallen and was blocking the sidewalk and an entire lane of traffic. This second log fell in the same spot I was walking the day before. Whoa. Could my vibes be causing a great collapse?

Day 165 of Isolation

Looking back on history, we can easily spot major events that changed daily life for us forever. The AIDS virus resulted in medical practitioners wearing gloves for even routine exams. September 11 transformed air travel. I have a theory that this Coronavirus will usher in a new level of teleworking, which will release the stranglehold of Middle-Eastern oil on the world and bring about.... WORLD PEACE. You heard it here first.

Day 166 of Isolation

Today's daily negotiation of When Mommy Will Wake Up happened at 7:37 AM.

> **Me, employs delay tactics:** Is your room clean?
>
> **Mary:** Yep.
>
> **Me:** Will you open the shades?
>
> **Mary:** [Flounces off.]

Me: [Rolls over.]

Mary, returns, dressed: Why aren't you up?

Me, chastened: Because you didn't open the shades?

Mary: I'm not in the mood for joking around.

Me: [Goes into bathroom.]

Mary: When are you going to get dressed?

Me: [Extended groan.]

Mary: Stop whining!

When your words come back to haunt you. Girl has a point.

Day 167 of Isolation

Morning walk and my daughter is balancing on a retaining wall *while* wearing rollerblades. Sad how my children are so timid, isn't it?

Day 168 of Isolation

Another masked excursion to Costco. Only took forty-five minutes today, including getting gas — no line to enter, no line for self check-out. That's a record.

I got a box of Kirkland Tequila Silver... and filled that box with ground beef, laundry detergent, paper sacks and a prescription we picked up. More's the pity.

Day 169 of Isolation

If I'm being honest, I dread the start of school. At this point, I'm not sure if my kids are bad at transitions, or I am. Either way, we hit our summer rhythm and changing to the Covid school rhythm will cause significant discomfort. I do not want to be out of comfort.

Of course, that transition is compounded by the fact that this will be a whole new version of learning. In the spring, the kids had ninety minutes of instruction Monday, Wednesday, and Friday mornings; they spent the rest of the time doing the assignments they received. At first, I thought teachers were going too easy on the students, but any greater burden would've flattened us. Now they plan a full day of school every day, so [logically] I fear we'll be pancakes by each day's end.

This is not to say that I have a better plan! Also, the teachers are doing a flat-out fantastic job. They impressed me with how well they transitioned their classroom management skills to the internet. I can't imagine how I will engage Mary to do her lessons. When Damien had six full-strength classes, keeping track of them all made his head spin.

I've been busy with, and tired from, getting the kids new school clothes. So much buying and taking back, because fitting rooms are not open. Mind you, they don't need the clothing to go to school, as they won't be *going* anywhere. No one suspended "growing" in the stay at home order, though, so needs must. In fact, I call them school clothes, but only two or three are actual clothing items. The rest are glorified workout gear, because why bother?

Buying school supplies was easy — we had pens, pencils, and paper in stock. They still have their district issued Chromebooks from spring, and I bought a 10-pack of styluses to go with.

No packed lunches is a perk.

I am eager for other adults to provide things for my kids to do at least part of the day — both are acting out their boredom in their own uniquely unpleasant ways.

Daze of Isolation

But the intense discomfort appears unavoidable and coping with that impending doom is draining me. Also, we're in the dog days of summer here. Heat kills my desire to cook, grocery shop, clean the house, or exercise, so all of those have fallen by the wayside. In summary, we have new clothes, school supplies, and sunshine. Focusing on positive.

Day 170 of Isolation

Tonight, on Star Trek, the crew snuck onto an enemy ship, and Captain Archer instructed them to "fan out" to search for their stolen antimatter, weapons, and food. Damien said, "I like when they say 'fan out' instead of 'split up.' It sounds so much safer." Proving that 14-year-olds can still be adorable. Next time we all go to Fred Meyer, and I divvy up the grocery list among us, I'm gonna say, "Fan out and search for our rations."

> **Patricia:** Antimatter on the Fred Meyer list? Just asking...
>
> **Me:** Yeah, our minivan runs on a warp drive, so I'll need to pick some of that up. #Iwish

Day 172 of Isolation

I triumphed in my protracted battle to manufacture slime. Behold! The perfect gelatinous mass.

Surviving Pandemic Motherhood on Diet Coke and a Prayer

> **Brian:** So how many attempts? And where are the other samples?
>
> **Me:** So many attempts. Months of attempts.

Day 174 of Isolation

I went out tonight, without children, to help with another church project, which is a surprise. Top Secret. Don't try to make me tell you, because I'm like a vault.[10] They were planning a photo shoot, so I got dressed up and made up, which is unusual nowadays, so I explained.

> **Me:** I'm headed out.
>
> **Jeff:** Have fun!
>
> **Me:** They're taking pictures, which is why I'm all fancy.

---

[10] I can't stand the pressure! We were packing up swag bags for our new book study, *The Emotionally Healthy Woman*, by Geri Scazzero. What? Of course I read it! Can't you tell?

Jeff: Gotcha.

Me: I didn't want you to think it was because I got a little sumthin' on the side...

Jeff: Yeah, that would've been my first thought.

Me: Cuz, you know, my Facebook memories said that seven years ago, a guy hit on me. So, I'm in demand.

Day 175 of Isolation

We pause on International Dog Day to recognize our pandemic champ: Abby. She never bickers, though we're all home all the time. She's up for every crazy idea we come up with, even super long car rides. She didn't complain when we repeatedly tried to drown her tennis ball in Puget Sound, hoping she would swim after it like she did when she was a pup. She doesn't call me a sissy when I wear a mask; she doesn't call me selfish if I don't. She doesn't mind who wins the election.

Day 176 of Isolation

Put the finishing touches on the sourdough cinnamon rolls I started two days ago. I left a lot of room for improvement. I messed up the autolyze. I omitted several stretch and folds. The dough rose too long and stayed too long in the fridge. I was meant to bring the dough to room temperature and returned it to the fridge instead. Despite all of that, we somehow managed to choke them down.

Surviving Pandemic Motherhood on Diet Coke and a Prayer

SUGAR FIXES EVERYTHING.

Day 178 of Isolation

We found a Sony Walkman on our family walk. Someone was going to miss their music, but I didn't come across anyone wearing a Members Only jacket or sporting a mullet, so we leaned the lost relic against a post and hope they are reunited.

Speaking of anomalies, Damien picked a bunch of grapes growing in the wild. That vine is a mystery — grapes don't grow wild in Washington. And check out that beautiful, de-braced grin.

The day's crowning achievement, though, is my first naturally leavened boule of sourdough. I have been using starter for months now, but almost all my recipes supplement with instant yeast, which seems like cheating. What can I say? I need sandwich bread! After all this utilitarian baking, going without yeast is like working without a net, but by late afternoon, I had two golden-brown artisan loaves of crusty yumminess. One of which went down our collective hatches right away. #breadhigh

Day 179 of Isolation

Got a cool present at the beach: crutches! Well, they weren't very cool. And they weren't a present, as I trust we'll pay a hefty bill.

I've had both hips replaced due to congenital hip dysplasia, and replacements carry an ongoing risk of dislocation. One is never to lift one's knee past 90°, nor cross one's leg over the midline of one's torso, and especially not at the same time. Which is what I did.

Basically, for the rest of my life, I should be moving as though I'm carrying a full-term baby. Knees and feet akimbo. Can't bend forward when rising from a chair. No high-knees, toe-touches, etc. However, I don't have any barriers to doing those things, like carrying a human inside, and sometimes I forget.

So, I was on the beach, I knew exactly what happened, and any movement was excruciating: even contracting the muscle to consider moving. I managed to lumber over on my side, and Jeff and I

Surviving Pandemic Motherhood on Diet Coke and a Prayer

agreed that we needed 911: That quarter mile to the parking lot was insurmountable, and the tide was coming in.

> **911 Dispatcher:** Just checking, ma'am. When you said the water was 6 feet away from you, was that sarcasm or is it really 6 feet away?
>
> **Me:** I'm glad you asked. Yes, the water's 6 feet away and gaining on me.

In fact, by the time the ambulance arrived, the [cold] water was lapping at my toes. Damien was waiting by the parking lot to direct the EMTs to our position, and suddenly we saw him running to us, carrying my back board, à la Baywatch. He was secretly thrilled, and I don't blame him. I bet he had the eye of every teen girl there.

He outran the EMTs, so Jeff and Damien and I cautiously rolled me onto the backboard, and then Jeff, Damien, and the EMTs carried me further up on the beach. Which was a relief, because the water had reached my booty by then. At that point, they recorded my medical history (significant) and started me on IV pain meds (also significant), because....

There was a longish ride to the nearest trauma center: we traveled the width of Whidbey Island, then hopped a ferry, then bounced along another twenty minutes to the hospital. Jeff followed in the car with the kids, and he was tickled to bypass the whole ferry line and drive straight on. They latched the gate behind us, and we were off.

I knew Jeff and the kids wouldn't be allowed into the hospital because of Covid-19, so I asked the EMT to let them inside the ambulance on the ferry. I hadn't had a chance to talk to them in all the bustle, and I hoped to reassure them a little. See? Mom's still laughing; no blood; no big deal.

Daze of Isolation

Even though it was a big deal. The EMT helped me rig up a sheet that I could loop around my leg to keep my hip immobilized. I had a death grip on that thing (which I referred to as "the reins") the whole ride.

Once we got to the ER, Jeff took the kids home, unpacked, showered everyone, picked up Taco Time and ate outside the hospital in solidarity with me. What a sweet guy I have, right?

My EMT besties wheeled me into a room, and they transferred me oh-so-gently to a bed, as I clutched my reins. I answered all the questions, and then...

> **Me:** This is probably the least of my worries, but the reason I was getting up off my beach towel was to go to the bathroom, and that was two hours ago, so...?
>
> **Nurse:** Oh, my! Yes — I'll find you a hot dog...

Alright, that wasn't the name she used. She returned with a next-gen catheter for women. (Photo not shown due to kinky appearance. You can Google Pure-wick.) They wedge a rubber hot-dog-shaped item between one's legs and hook the other end up to a vacuum cleaner. I could not relax enough, what with the fear of any movement and the Hot Dog. So, my bladder remained full for four hours while all the other stuff was happening. Nonetheless, if you ever wind up in this situation, check out the hot dog. Sure beats the old technology.

The doctor confirmed my dislocated joint via x-ray, and they put me under. Anesthetized is my favorite way to have joints relocated. Once I woke up, I was all better. He said the joint didn't go back in without a fight. The first procedure they tried didn't work, so they had to do a "Captain Morgan." You'll have to Google that, too, as I find I don't want to know. The doctor prescribed crutches but said I could walk on the leg "as tolerated."

This afternoon, I was walking around without the crutches, and Jeff scolded me. He thinks my definition of "as tolerated" is way too liberal.

The dog is sure my crutches are Devil Sticks and won't come near me until I set them down. She shares my definition of "as tolerated."

I meet with my new orthopedic surgeon Wednesday, as the wonderful doc who did both my hips retired last year. The new guy will tell me if anything else must be done, or if they can let me off with a stern warning and lots of physical therapy. Oh, please; Oh, please a stern warning...

Day 180 of Isolation

Though yesterday included six hours in the ER, the show must go on, amiright? Jeff had major deadlines at work. I had a podiatrist appointment. The dog had a pebble lodged so deeply in her paw that we couldn't dislodge it. The only opening at the veterinarian was at the same time (but not same city) as mine. Typical.

So, on my first day post-dislocation, Mary and I dropped Abby at the vet, drove to my doctor's office, picked up pebble-free pup, and went home. But after that, I totally rested. P.S. Both the dog and I were getting our "paws" worked on at the same time. Giggle.

SEPTEMBER

SPENTEMBER

Our state lifted restrictions enough for small groups of people to gather together, wearing masks, outdoors. While the weather was still fair, we took the opportunity to visit our parents and siblings. School started... such as it was. Smoke from distant fires put more restrictions on our restrictions.

● ●

Day 181 of Isolation

Tomorrow is our first day of school, 3rd and 9th grade, all online for now. I'm nervous because it was stressful in the spring, when they had a reduced workload and gentle grading. Now, they're aiming for the typical workload, regular grading.

Lawd, have mercy.

Many of us are spurring ourselves and each other on with "You got this, girl!" or " I got this! " This is not a criticism: that is 2020's rallying cry.

For me, though, I do not got this, and I haven't gotten it for 181 days, and I accept that. This whole thing is sorta... ungettable. Everyone is feeling the pinch; everyone's emotions are about a hair's breadth from the surface.

So, I will try to stay flexible; accept that I'm writing this at 1:43 am because of an insomnia flare up; expect that I'll be crying on some school days. When I have insomnia, I fire up my Kindle and reassure myself with my Bible reading for that day. I felt myself relax when I opened today's reading for parents of extreme kids, titled:

God's Got This

Day 182 of Isolation

Jeff and I met my new orthopedic surgeon today. He said the likely reason my hip dislocated was that the joint is over twenty years old, and the plastic cup has worn away, making it unstable. Not because I was cavalier about how I moved. No stern warnings.

My choices are:

Do nothing. Maintain post-surgical precautions. Gamble my hip won't slip out again, though my hip will dislocate more easily now that it popped out once already. Lovely.

Replace the worn part via surgery. Five days in hospital; six weeks on crutches.

Yeah, I think they're awesome choices, too. Doesn't matter, though, because no way am I going to be laid up for that long while the kids are on house arrest, so I will simply take my chances with option A.

Here's how young my new orthopedic surgeon is:

> **Me:** The pain was terrible until they put it back, and then it felt like nothing happened. It was like Mel Gibson's shoulder dislocating in *Lethal Weapon*, then POP! He was back to beating up the bad guys.
>
> **Doctor:** [Expressionless.] Huh. I'm not familiar with that movie.

It was more than *one* movie. It was more than a *movie*. It was an era.

Day 183 of Isolation

Yesterday, in spite of recent medical stressors, I made it until 4:47 PM without any yelling. Today, I yelled some things before school, during school, during lunch... Second of eSchool meets PMS meets packing for vacation tomorrow. Can't stop yelling. Yelled while typing these words. Why can't people listen to what I say and do it?

Day 184 of Isolation

Gaaaahhh! Flip flipping flippety flip flipping flipper flipped fliiiippppp! Flip. Flip. 8:36 AM. Failed my no yelling efforts. Spectacularly. I would like to speak to the manager.

[Spotify plays *Come and Lay Your Burdens Down* by Jamie Klimmet]

I guess I am speaking to the manager, and he is speaking to me. Prob'ly gonna be some embarrassingly loud singing happening now. Maybe some ugly crying.

Day 185 of Isolation

Oh, my, Lord. This is the first time the kids played on a playground in six months. They played together! My stress drained away as I saw Mary running off to climb on all the things. In most of our travels, playground equipment is roped off with warnings and bright yellow caution tape.

This park is at Percival Landing in Olympia, also famous for the lifelike statues and art installations spread throughout the boardwalk area. I think we found them.

Daze of Isolation

KARATE KID'S MOM

MOM-A-THONER

MOM RESCUES SON

Surviving Pandemic Motherhood on Diet Coke and a Prayer

THE LOST ART OF CURTSY

Day 186 of Isolation

Had a nightmare last night that I tested positive for COVID-19. On the weekend when we're visiting all our loved ones in the south. This crap is getting to me.

Day 187 of Isolation

We got home from our vacation around 3 PM, and Mary helped unpack, so I had nothing left to do by 4 PM.

So, I got out some meat to thaw, and I saw the bones set aside for broth, so I started the broth.

Behind the bones in the freezer was the bag of stale bread cubes, and next to that were the sub-par blackberries, so I mixed up a double batch of Blackberry French Toast for the morning.

Underneath the bones, bread, and berries were the ice cube trays, so I emptied and refilled those.

I remembered I was out of hot cocoa mix, so I measured twenty individual serve boxes of that.

By then, it was time to start making dinner, and that was how I did nothing for two hours.

Day 188 of Isolation

The good news is, I did not yell so far today. (12:33 PM PDT)

The bad news is, my daughter made up for me on our walk.

I kept saying to myself, "At least I'm not yelling. It's a start."

I came home to discover the teacher was out sick, so I could've slept in, walked at a leisurely pace, and most likely avoided the whole scene.

I'm yelling inside right now.

Day 189 of Isolation

Real conversations I have with myself:

> **Me, disapprovingly:** You're going to buy *another* soda?
>
> **Myself:** Hey — back off! I'm doing the best I can.
>
> **Me:** I think you're phoning it in.
>
> **Myself, stymied by this truth. Then:** Sometimes, phoning it in *is* the best I can do.

At that, Me gives Myself a hug, and we drive off into the haze to pick up an ice-cold, large, Diet Coke.

> **Fran:** Overruling yourself is a clever tactic.
>
> **Me:** Myself can't help but agree with you.
>
> **Jerre:** My kids call it "the mommy juice".

Day 190° of Isolation

Well, it's not 190° here. Just short of 90°, actually, but many acres of Washington are hitting hundreds of degrees as wildfires rage. A smoke cloud many miles wide is about to pass through, which means closed windows, no air conditioning. Even under those circumstances, we're better off than the many evacuees. What a strange year — and I mean that in the worst way.

I helped Mary last night to make her own schedule out of Legos — red for academics, white for snack, yellow for playtime, etc. Trying to help her to see and feel time. Lego Schedule may have worked, because today was our first decent day of 3rd grade.

That gave me a little breather from teaching, so can I mention that I walked into the dark garage Tuesday morning, and something feathered across the top of my hair? Like when you walk through a curtained doorway. "Funny," I thought, "there are no curtains in that doorway... Waaaait a minute..."

I turned around, and as I feared, there was an 8-legged brute on the ceiling under which I had passed. Doubtless rubbing his fuzzy paws in glee. High-pitched squealing and "get it off me!" dance ensued.

Day 191 of Isolation

The school emailed parents that we'd be responsible to cover Sexual Health and HIV Education, and I kept it as a reminder. I "snoozed" that message all summer. Will my son be more scarred if I skip those lessons or more scarred receiving those lessons from his mom? Hmmm...

> **Amber:** What are they going to foist off on you next?
>
> **Me:** Football. I'm laughing as I picture telling Damien I'm his new coach.

Day 192 of Isolation

The sky is yellow; so, another day of trying to explain why my Social Butterfly will be caged. But we're better off than past summers, because what can they do to us? Cancel Zoom school?

Day 193 of Isolation

Ladies and Gentlemen, this is a clear mandate to go shopping. Which is how we got new bathmats this weekend. Silky, fluffy ones. Upon which my son is obsessed with leaving handprint designs.

Day 194 of Isolation

My attitude is in the dumper. The outdoors is draped in smoke — like a cloudy day, if the clouds could hurt you. Sun looks like the moon. Windows sealed to keep out the smoke; fan off to keep out the smoke, kids inside to keep the smoke out of them. 76° indoors. Damp with sweat all day, and I can't shake the feeling that we four are re-breathing our own filth. Weather forecasts this through the end of the week.

> **Damien:** Hey, Mama — how you doin'?
>
> **Me:** I'm whining.

Daze of Isolation

In my head, the whining is louder, and with more swearing. I may be screaming in my heart.[11]

Day 195 of Isolation

MAKING THE BEST OF IT.

It was Mary's picture day at school. Here she is, waiting on the "6 feet apart" line, with face mask, holding a "thank you" sign she made for the teachers. Covid Picture Day is a once in a lifetime opportunity for parents to decorate their kids immediately before the photos are taken — no recess, lunch, P.E. or "I took it off" to mess things up. Truly: a control freak's dream. I will have photographic evidence of braids!

---

[11] Social media dubbed "Please scream inside your heart" 2020's motto, referring to an overly literal translation of Fujiyama roller-coaster wording.

Day 196 of Isolation

Authorities downgraded most of Washington's air quality to "Unhealthy" from "Very Unhealthy." We are on the edge of our seats. Can "Unhealthy for Sensitive Populations" be far behind?

Day 197 of Isolation

One of Mary's assignments read: Use the text tool to type 3 words that describe you.

She typed: Candy Unicorn Pumpkin

Yeah — that sounds about right.

Day 198 of Isolation

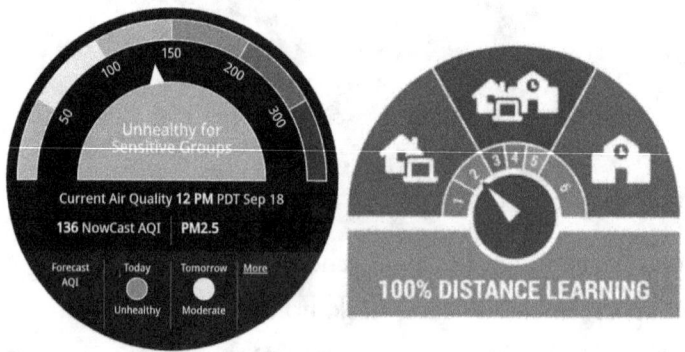

Our daily lives are inordinately governed by these little graphics. Even the children check them, waiting for the colors to change and the pointers to move. Both kids went outdoors at 2 PM for the first time in seven days. They were so excited. They didn't mind that they got rained on.

Day 199 of Isolation

We met my parents and my aunt from Illinois at Point No Point Lighthouse. The kids are always so wonderful outside! They act like the *car* is too small for the two of them. The *house* is too small for the two of them. A *ferry* is too small for the two of them. But the *entire* out of doors is just the right size for them to be friendly.

Day 200 of Isolation

The first day of academics for 3rd and 9th graders today. Classes have been comprised of lighthearted, get-to-know-each-other activities up to now. Mary completed a small amount of the morning assignments, and then went on strike until we surrendered and told her she could do her schoolwork or go to bed early. She went to bed early, and it was for the best.

Day 201 of Isolation

When is it my turn to kick and scream and throw things? I don't get a turn? Sigh. Well, at least I get two chocolate chip cookies. This is how parents gain weight.

Day 202 of Isolation

Be careful what you wish for. Eight years ago today, I wished "National Wear Your Sweats to Church Day" was a thing. Now, National Wear Your Sweats to Church Day = Sunday

> **Amber:** So, it's your fault, then?
>
> **Me:** So it would seem. Though if this was some major conspiracy, it was fomented by the makers of video conferencing software...
>
> **Amber:** ...and Toilet Paper.

Day 203 of Isolation

Yesterday, an "asynchronous learning" day, was passable. I thought we might survive online school. Made some plans, stormed some brains. Today, we're back to raging. What? What's so different about this day? Is it the diagnostic testing? Can she not last past lunchtime? Is it a backlash of Zoom, much like how TV turns both my kids into monsters? What the actual... Heck?

Day 204 of Isolation, 6:22 AM

For much of the night, I thought I detected extra breathing in our room, and sure enough, there was baby girl, curled asleep in our corner chair. We are now approaching "menagerie" in here, what with husband, dog, daughter, and self.

Daze of Isolation

Suddenly, Mary stands, mutters, "Can't sleep," and tromps down the hall to her room.

Which is ironic, because somewhere around 2 AM this morning, she came to our room complaining she couldn't possibly sleep in *her* room.

Day 205 of Isolation

Mary was doing her math diagnostic test. The question read: if there are 35 cookies and 5 kids, how many does each kid receive? This problem required division, which they did not cover in class yet. Multiplication was only touched on in two lessons last June. She arrived at the correct answer by brute force addition. She is quite impressive. I'm glad I got a peek of that — it helps to remind me of the amazing little girl who lives here.

P.S. She drew it out on paper. There were five happy faces, with a "7" below each face. Yeah, I guess I'd be happy, too, if I got seven cookies.

Day 206 of Isolation

One reason school has been so difficult is that Mary's least favorite thing is penmanship. Unfortunately, almost every subject is writing assignment, for example:

Math: Copy the instructions for math game into your math journal.

Science: Play video and write three observations about octopuses in your science journal.

Reading: Read for twenty minutes (her next least favorite thing to do, by the way) and fill out your reading journal about what you read.

Writing: Write five awesome things about yourself...

By the time she gets to writing, she's written well past her point of exhaustion!

I tweaked all these instructions and obtained permission from the teacher for her to type most of her assignments. I could've just told her the news, but I couldn't pass up the opportunity to do a little sales job:

> **Me:** Mary, I think that you don't like writing very much, because you think it means using a pencil to make words. But writing is how we tell stories, and you love telling stories! Mr. C. says you can tell your stories with a pencil and paper, or you can type your stories. Which one do you want to use?
>
> **Mary, excited:** Typing!
>
> **Me:** Excellent choice! Today in writing, we can practice voice typing.

So, during writing, we covered the basics of voice typing, such as don't bury the computer's microphone in the carpet; don't say one word over and over, say your whole sentence for context; computers do not listen better if you speak louder....

Result? She wrote a very short story by herself, and she was even excited to read the finished product to me. Only took three weeks to arrive at that point, but who's counting?

Day 207 of Isolation

We're finally seeing the world in living color again. Thanks for nothing, Smoke. My bed is dappled with fall sunshine on a Sunday afternoon. I'm tracking how the Seahawks are faring by the sound of cheers from son and husband downstairs, as well as fans around the neighborhood through the open window. I'm reclining with a juicy thriller while I babysit a tedious Windows 10 update. Giggles and chatter of Mary and her friends playing in the woods is also floating in through the window. Fireworks from across the valley tell me when the game is over. Thanks for everything, Sunshine.

Day 208 of Isolation

Had the first almost-tolerable day of online school today. Followed by a Zoom Bible Study. Followed by a prickly fight with spouse. I had, quite admirably, put a tremendous amount of effort and energy into Number One Daughter, and neglected, snapped at, and otherwise hurt Number One Husband. I can see why that did not fly. Re-tooling. Again.

Day 209 of Isolation

After the kids were in bed, my grown-up kid came in to show me a bright, coppery penny...

> **Jeff:** No matter how old I get, it makes me so happy to find a shiny penny...
>
> **Me, thinking:** Yeah, that is pretty adorable.
>
> **Jeff, continues:** ... It's freshly minted. 2020!
>
> **Me, thinking:** Now I want to smash it with a sledgehammer.
>
> This is why I don't own a sledgehammer.

Surviving Pandemic Motherhood on Diet Coke and a Prayer

Day 210 of Isolation

    I see a bad sun rising. This better not stick around, or I will lose my you-know-what!

OCTOBER

OCTOVID

Washington Covid cases were on the rise, weather was on the decline. We were settling into academic routines, sorta. Nothing was awful, but the constant low-level deprivation was a grind for us all.

●●●●●●●●●●●●●●●●●●●●

Day 211 of Isolation

On my morning walks, I scroll through my email, review class schedules, and sometimes catch up on longer articles. I'm on the mailing list for the Family Dinner Project, which helps people live out the "family that eats together, stays together" adage. Today's message intro described families trying to find the silver lining in this pandemic and I rolled my eyes as I thought, "This, I gotta see!"

As I suspected, there were a lot of people nattering on about all the quality family time they're having, and how their family is cooking together, and their daughter's making brownies every week... And then there was Amy. Amy: you are my people.

"We now watch shows at dinner. We are together ALL DAY. We talk ALL DAY. At dinner time, I just need a d**** break..." — Amy, single parent of two.

Day 212 of Isolation

Dad reads Bible stories to Mary each night. Sometimes I'm there, too.

> **Daddy:** What did Jesus give to his friends?
>
> **Me, enthusiastically:** Covid-19!
>
> **Mary, disgusted:** No! He gave his friends *bread*.

Jeff loves me.

Day 213 of Isolation

After a week of trying and failing, I managed to update Windows 10. The computer toiled through the night at our bedside. I could tell Jeff was thrilled our laptop remained lit up for the duration. I guess Microsoft assumed, being stuck at home during a pandemic, we'd nothing better to do than babysit our computer for 12 hours.

Day 214 of Isolation

Instead of Covid-19, we should write it Covid-XIX. Like the Super Bowl. We could pretend this is a game. That we could win. And earn a ring, and a trophy, and sponsorship deals.

Day 215 of Isolation

Whenever someone brings up "self-care", my brain goes straight to bubble baths, a gripping novel, and sleeping, in that order. My girlfriends and I were chatting about self-care recently, and they suggested exercise and eating right, which had not occurred to me. Unless by "eating right," they meant eating Oreos. While taking a bubble bath.

Daze of Isolation

What never crossed my mind was self-care via what I *say* to myself. Like:
- I'm doing the best I can.
- My job is to be content myself and give my kids tools to succeed in life, but I'm not responsible for their happiness.
- Adults do not need to be rescued.
- I can forgive myself and others for mistakes.

Being kind to myself in my head is so soothing. I've also had some success with clapping on some clunky headphones and blasting my music to drown out the little one being responsible for her own happiness.

I asked my friends what they do, and here is what they said:

Shop by myself • Brush my hair • Throw math book into the forest • Declutter • Garden • Paint at night, when the house is quiet • Do one productive thing for my career • Snuggle in a blanket with a loaded Kindle • Exercise • Try not to overeat • Binge Netflix • Bathe in essential oils • Dance • Yoga • Go to bed early

> **Dawn:** I'm not supposed to say Fireball, right?
>
> **Me:** As long as it doesn't cause worse problems. Like it would for me, a woman of very little restraint. See also: Diet Coke.

Day 216 of Isolation

I had two Covid 19 milestones today.

1. Lost patience with Mary, telling her in a not-very-nice tone to draw an array of 4 x 5 like her teacher asked, then a firmer "NO!" as she threatened to scribble with a marker on her math workbook. Which is when a grown-up voice came over the computer, saying, "Ehlers family: you are not muted..." Her teacher is very tactful.

2. Prepped Mary and the laptop for Zoom Taekwondo and was running a bubble bath when Jeff darted in exclaiming, "We can't log in!" I threw on my robe and rushed downstairs to the PC to fix it. That's when I realized Damien hooked it up while Jeff was finding me, and the woman with crazy hair and a white bathrobe on the display was me.

So, umm. I'm famous.

Day 217 of Isolation

On Wednesday nights, we pile in the car and head to prayer meeting. Jeff and I take turns watching Mary while the other joins the praying and Damien goes to youth group. It was my turn to pray for people, and I did so, fervently. Some of you fine people by name, even.

A couple of people there mentioned that they pray for us, and I'm so grateful because we need it. Prayer is well-suited to these jumbled up times, because... What the heck else can we do for each other? Can't throw a party, can hardly visit, can't go to our health club; online school, online Sunday school, online church. Can't give a friend a hug; can't give them a smile. But I can pray. It was heartening to be away from the daily grind and surrounded by all the praying.

Day 218 of Isolation

I did this. I haven't had acrylic nails in over five years. I stopped because money was tight, and thanks to Jeff's hard work and God's bountiful results, I can do them again. That may sound sappy, but Jeff continued to work hard amid disappointments and job changes. Finally, this year his efforts are paying off.

Daze of Isolation

In the interim, I did my nails myself. It blows. It was all: chemical stink annoying spouse, needing re-dos thrice weekly, nail stickers slipping off in the dishwater... In spite of all that work, there was always the one or two nails that broke and ruined the effect. I researched what to do to keep them intact, and one perky blog post read that one should not try to use one's fingernails for screwdrivers. What? That's a major benefit of being a woman! Having ten handy tools at the end of your fingers...

Now, my fingernails are back to being armor plated. Also, full disclosure: I have a lifelong habit of picking and scratching at my skin, and these lovely nails make picking anything much more difficult. Declawed, if you will.

Those were the perks I knew about, but when my new friend finished making my nails purty, she gave me a hand and shoulder massage! What do you suppose I did to deserve that? The deal sure didn't include that five years ago! I sure wasn't going to ask. #selfcare

Day 219 of Isolation

Guess what we did? We went to the bus stop! To pick up library books! Yes, it was the highlight of Mary's day! No, I can't stop typing exclamation points!

As soon as I reminded Mary that it was library book pickup day, she said, "I *knew* there was going to be something good today!" how I got her to complete music class. She insisted on taking her school backpack to carry the books — the first time she'd worn it since March.

In search of Library Bus

She was not alone — kids from all over the neighborhood paraded to the bus stop for their books, and we were all a little giddy to be around fresh humans. Keep in mind, we have books — we have a subscription to digital picture books, and I check out books from the county library, too. We went for the people.

Day 220 of Isolation

Allow me to introduce you to Flower 2, a.k.a. Slinky. Mary named the first caterpillar she took in Flower, because she found him near a flower. Unfortunately, she wanted to take Flower everywhere with her to show him to everyone. Flower rolled himself in a ball from the trauma, and never recovered.

I am averse to pets of any size dying, so when she found this one, I said she could only keep him on condition that he stay put on the kitchen counter next to the ant habitat.

According to Mary, Slinky is a Woolly Bear caterpillar, and will turn into a tiger moth if we play our cards right.

Slinky is far more entertaining than I anticipated. For one thing, he eats like crazy! We put a forest in there for him one night, and he defoliated every stem by the next morning. I gained a fresh understanding of Eric Carle's picture book, The Very Hungry Caterpillar.

For another: the feet. I added several sticks for Slinky to climb on, and my favorite is when he hangs upside down from the stick, so I can gaze at his tiny feet clinging to it. See them?

Day 221 of Isolation

No fitting rooms at Value Village has turned clothes shopping into a shell game.

Trip 1 to Value Village, last week: Bought Mary a raincoat. Came home. Went to hang up raincoat, only to find the raincoat I bought last year and stored for when she got to this size. Now, I will need to go back and buy something else, because they only do exchanges. No problem — I always "need" something there.

Trip 2, this morning: I took both kids to our favorite VV, which is a little further away, but with nicer stuff. I found a few things for them, and a lovely, non-rickety ironing board for me. I had a 50% off coupon for pants, but I didn't find any. No problem: I would still save money by returning Mary's coat... Except I neglected to bring the stupid coat.

Trip 3, now: I go to another VV, because my pants coupon expires today. Of course. I find several sets of pajamas for Mary, and a pair of pants for me. I have the coat from Trip 1, and some little thing from Trip 2 that didn't work out (not the lovely ironing board: she's a keeper). I'm all set! All I need is my receipt from Trip 1...

Only I seem to have cleaned out my purse recently and did not leave the receipt. Gah! I prepare to throw myself on the mercy of the clerk, who is dressed as a very convincing Velma from Scooby Doo, and she comes through for me. She refunds the coat by looking it up on my account — yay! I'm so excited that I forget to use my 50% off coupon. Zoinks!

No matter: the pants don't fit anyway. So, sometime in the next 14 days: Trip 4... (Would anyone like a picture of the ironing board?)

Day 222 of Isolation

Miserable. There are few days that go by that I don't think, "I can *not* do this." Don't know how to help my children; scarcely know how to help myself.

Day 223 of Isolation, approximately 2:23 AM

The good news is there was no actual fire. The bad news is there was a piercing fire *alarm* for a few long minutes.

> **Me, hitting Jeff repeatedly:** Get up, get up, get up!
> I may have said it a few more times.
>
> **Jeff, already moving:** What?
> Wishes wife would stop hitting him.
>
> **Son:** What *was* that? [Insert plausible explanation]
> A fire woulda' been cool.
>
> **Daughter:** That hurt my ears! I better sleep in your room in case it happens again.
> Girlfriend, it rings in every room...
>
> **Dog:** I may be going deaf, but I can still smell, and there ain't no fire. I'll chill on the bed while you all go nuts.

So, Fire Drill 2020 is a wrap.

Day 224 of Isolation

Same as Day 222: miserable.

Tuesday, Day 223, was decent. So, I asked myself: what was different about Tuesday? Was it the middle of the night fire alarm? Was it because we finished school early to go buy a new bike? As in, "You can only go with me to collect your new bike if you're done with school." That was probably it. Which is cool, because buying a new bike every day is so repeatable.

This is not hell, not by a long shot: we do find a way to laugh and giggle most days. But there is plenty of weeping and gnashing of teeth.

Day 225 of Isolation

Here's how I got my daughter to join her online math class. After getting a series of timeouts, the Zoom call became more attractive. So, she snuck downstairs to snatch her computer and join Zoom while she was supposed to be in timeout. I pretended not to catch her because she was doing what I wanted in the first place.

How's that for Positive Parenting? Pfft.

I mean, the bike only cost $30. Buying a new one every day doesn't sound so bad right about now.

Day 226 of Isolation

School laptop screen is broken. Details are sketchy — something about carrying it, then tripping and somehow stepping on it. No words.

Day 227 of Isolation

My body is doing unexpected things — going through The Change, as they say. Which is caused by a decrease in hormones and appears to result in very stable weight. I'm not losing; I'm not gaining. This is unheard-of for me — I yo-yo up and down five pounds depending on what time of the month it is.

Now, for weeks: the same. It's quite pleasant.

This must be what it's like to be a man.

> **Heather:** I have decided to stop aging. I will have none of it.
>
> **Me:** You're making the right choice.
>
> **Heather:** It feels right.

Day 228 of Isolation

I've been losing my temper on our Saturday morning walks, often ending up with me tramping off by myself while Jeff wrangles the children. This is caused by some combination of Taciturn Teen, little Chatty Kathy, lady hormones and politics. Today, though, I'm gonna go ahead and blame it on these hallucinogenic mushrooms we found. I did not ingest any, but still: that's my story and I'm sticking to it.

Day 229 of Isolation

I appreciate my friends nearby who voted by mail, and I particularly appreciate the ones who posted a photo of their ballot envelope...

Because Mary came running downstairs during her school Zoom call, insisting that we find a red and white envelope that came in the mail. A very important envelope! We need to work on the red and white envelope!

That red and white envelope would have defeated me if not for my voting friends. Our county's ballots come in lavender and white envelopes. Her teacher must be from the red and white county, and I only knew there were other colors because of the pictures. Social media put out one of fifty fires that threaten me on any given day. I'll take what I can get.

Day 230 of Isolation

Covid school has proven to me that the reasons children submit to school have little to do with an unquenchable desire to learn.

Kids go to school to be with friends. They agree to math, reading, and writing because of PE, recess, and lunch. They work on the assignments because there is nothing more interesting to do in the room. They behave due to peer pressure and friendly competition.

If teachers and parents manage to instill an unquenchable desire to learn by the time they graduate, it's a minor miracle.

Day 231 of Isolation

Of course, kids *are* born with an unquenchable thirst for play, and Mary does not want to play alone. Ever.

A typical youngest child. Who lives with three oldest children. Who learned to entertain themselves as toddlers, and now still do many things *by themselves*.

The other day, Mary and I did some things together in the morning. After that, Dad took her out to play basketball for a while, followed by hours of Sushigo. (Jeff is the most playful among us.) After she exhausted our playing resources, she bounced upstairs to ask brother if he would play. He said no, to which she replied with complete sincerity, "Come *on* Damien — you're my last hope!

Day 232 of Isolation

I can accept that our belongings will wear out over time, but I contend that the garage door opener, ice maker, vacuum cleaner, microwave, and (this just in) the printer over 232 days constitutes higher than average breakage.

Anecdotal evidence suggests that electrical devices can contract Covid-19.

> **Amber:** The microwave again? Has to be gremlins. They travel through the electrical conduits.
>
> **Me:** It's Covid, I tell you: the microwave got it, recovered, then got it again. Look at my data...

Day 233 of Isolation

Our new printer arrived, and the IT department (me) worked after hours to configure it. I consider it to be a sign of the times that I have our Wi-Fi password memorized. The password is thirty-two randomized, alphanumeric characters, but I type it in at least twice a week setting up all the things.

Day 234 of Isolation

Let's talk about Halloween, Covid-style. Our congregation is doing a drive thru harvest carnival, and we're going, and you can come, too! Anyone is welcome. The parking lot will be set up with games, candy, social distance: the works.

Which brings me to my next point: costumes. I maintain that we only need a costume from the waist up. I mean, drive thru festival means no one sees below the car windowsill, right? Our school events are drive-thru (Damien) and Zoom party (Mary) — also waist up.

In conclusion, I propose all Halloween costumes should be half-off. Who's with me?

Day 235 of Isolation

Our pastors announced today that services will be in-person again starting on November 22. Around here, that date is known as "my birthday." The pastors refer to it as "regathering," but I'm gonna call it my birthday party...

Day 236 of Isolation

Wait! What? There's no one else in my house? Ohmigosh, ohmigosh. I'm putting on some music. Loud, loud music... If you can't feel it, it's not. Loud. Enough.

As I was listening to the loud music, it occurred to me that we have a splendid, long, hardwood floor hallway. Soon it was looking like a cross between Risky Business and Mrs. Doubtfire up in here. Only with pants on.

Day 237 of Isolation

Sure, I realize waterfowl are not as racy as a cougar[12], but I was chased by a flock of ducks today. Perhaps I will be famous now.

---

[12] Were you one of the 7 million people who viewed the video of a man chased by mama cougar protecting cubs?

Daze of Isolation

Day 238 of Isolation

Due to many of our appliances catching their death of Covid-19, we are now about to be overrun by large-ish trash. I am dedicating this week to carting it off to the most useful place. Here's my list — y'all think I can wrap this up this week? Because I am so ready to have my garage back.[13]

- ☐ Batteries to Lowes
- ☐ Bike rack on Craigslist
- ☐ Bike to sharingwheels.org
- ☐ CPAP machines to reseller [if accepting in spite of germs]
- ☐ Expired meds to police department
- ☑ iMac to Apple, where 14-year-old computers retire.
- ☑ iPod to Apple, from taking frustrations out on electronics
- ☑ Kindle to Amazon. [Got $5 for it!]
- ☐ Plastic bags to store [an easy one!]
- ☑ Printer to Goodwill

---

[13] I did not finish by the end of that week, nor even by the time of this printing. Stupid propane canisters and old sneakers.

- ☑ Puzzles and math books to friend
- ☐ Running shoes to recycle
- ☐ Spent CFL bulb, propane cans to hazmat drop-off
- ☐ Vacuum, non-working, to...?
- ☐ Weighted blanket to another friend.

Chelsea: Did you...alphabetize this? I think I love you.

Me: *blush* Yes. Yes, I did.

Day 239 of Isolation

I don't mean to brag, but I wore pants with zippers three days this week, and a skirt on Sunday! You know what this means, right? Yup: I am *winning* Covid.

Day 240 of Isolation

That feeling when lunch is two hours overdue, and you're well into being hangry, and you bite into a handful of hot McDonald's French fries... #freefriesfriday

Day 241 of Isolation

Somehow, I thought that the first time I placed an insurance claim for one of my kids hitting a car, it would be for my son, who is older and closer to driving an actual vehicle.

Nope. It was my eight-year-old daughter, who went down a steep hill on her bike without braking, could not stop, and ran into the back of a parked car hard enough to crack their taillight and scratch up the paint on their quarter panel.

Her (three-week-old) bicycle is unrideable.

She's fine. She doesn't think so, but considering the damage to the vehicle and bike, her sore front tooth is practically a relief to us. Dentist said to come in Monday for an x-ray.

Daze of Isolation

We had scarcely left the neighborhood with brother in charge at home when she called us. Based on the timing, she hit the back of the car about three milliseconds after I said to Jeff, "Hey! This is like a date!"

Screaming in my heart. And a little screaming out loud, too.

NOVEMBER

NO ENDER

November in Seattle is often a gloomy month, marking the end of crisp, fall days and the beginning of flood season. In our case, November also turned our fragile reopenings into reclosings as cases spiked to all-time highs.

● ●

Day 242 of Isolation

I had a clean house. All clean at the same time. Here's what happened:

I mentioned that our Saturday morning walks have degraded in quality. Jeff and I still think a stroll is a great family activity, but the kids consider it to be a form of torture.

So, I told them we will be pausing walks. Instead, we'll be doing projects Saturday mornings. This weekend: cleaning the house. My thinking was that I tried a pleasant activity, and it kept ending up unpleasantly. Now, we'll try something unpleasant, but no matter what, it will end with something pleasant: a clean house.

Yes, I did snap at each kid once or twice, and they did grouse and complain, same as on our walks.

Be that as it may, when Saturday was over, my whole house was clean. Next weekend: the yard.

After that: the cars.

After that: the house will need it again.

After that, a walk might not sound so bad. Or else I'll adjust to having a clean house.

Day 243 of Isolation

It was just a meltdown, like many others: it started over something little. I thought I was being reasonable; daughter disagreed. I stood firm; she attacked things to convince me to budge.

It simply hit me harder than usual. She opened the linen closet and pulled out every towel, every sheet...and every heirloom quilt tucked away inside. Quilts that Jeff's and my grandmothers spent hours snipping, piecing, and stitching. They put them together out of deep love and deep practicality to bless their family and keep them warm.

One of them went on my bed when I had my first hip surgery at age five. One went to college with me. One blessed our new marriage; one warmed our new house. Several came when each grandma eventually passed on. The quilts connect me to them in a way that is visceral as a daughter, mom and craftswoman. I miss those women, and this is how I hold on to their memories. And she ripped them out, stomped on them, and poured liquid soap all over them.

I cried the entire time I was putting them away. Partly because of what happened. Partly out of grief for the lost dream of a little girl's room decorated with the same quilts that covered my bed. You might think, "You're lucky she didn't use markers or scissors!" Oh, that's not luck, friend. Scissors and markers are kept in a secure location. Because that's our reality. And sometimes it makes me cry.

Day 244 of Isolation (Election Day)

Soon, we'll find out if we're gonna have a new president or a used president. Some of us voted for the one guy, and some voted for the other guy, and some simply voted against the one. Or against the other. Whatever happens, can we not call any voter stupid? Let us stay united by assuming that we all had our reasons, and we all did our best, and now let's be neighbors again. Our future does not depend on one man. Except Jesus, and he'll still be in office tomorrow.

Day 245 of Isolation

More ado about quilts... I don't know how God speaks to you in your distress, but here's how he works in mine. I sat in my car in the rain, putting my feelings from Quilt Day on Facebook.

The first thing that came to mind was how that day started. Mary came into my room, complaining of sleeplessness. Daylight saving said it was 5:30, but her body still said it was 6:30. She crawled into bed with us and proceeded to run her fingers through my hair. That felt heavenly. Then she gave me a back massage. That felt like getting a massage from a very determined butterfly. She gave me hugs and tucked me into my blankets.

She left after a while to play with her remote-control car. God reminded me that she is the most generous person I know. She's cheerful, funny, smart, cute, and strong. Her emotions often spin into a tornado, too unruly for her to handle, leaving a path of destruction behind. We can learn how to handle those. I learned that last phrase in my Bible study Monday night.

About that time, screens full of comfort flooded in from the living women in my world. Frankly, I wasn't always able to cry things out, nor to receive comfort when given. That's God, too, because I treasured all the kind words and emojis.

"And what *about* those quilters?" God nudged. They didn't make fragile, lacy blankies. Those blankets were built to be strong and to last. They exactly reflected the women who made them. Among our grandmas were two women who outlived their sons. Several who lived with alcoholic and/or mean husbands. All of them saw intense financial difficulty. One was an adoptee like my two. They certainly shed their share of tears! After that, they got up and went back to work, taking care of bidness.

Which is what I did. It seemed to me the best business would be baking. So, I put up some sourdough loaves which will go in the oven shortly, some lemon poppy-seed muffins, dinner, and a Pear Plum Crumble[14], seasoned with cardamom. Because I had ripe pears and plums, and any day's the right day to use cardamom. #justkeepswimming

Day 246 of Isolation

I go for a walk most mornings, and I park in the same parking spot. Every time. Except if Jeff's driving. At this point, I think I own that spot. This morning, a lady parked with her tires on the white border of My Spot (the horror!), but I decided to go ahead and wedge my car into it.

For one thing, it's mine.

For another, experience tells me she won't stay long.

---

[14] https://theviewfromgreatisland.com/baking-up-a-storm-with-cardamom-pears-and-plums/

Daze of Isolation

She didn't make it easy for me. She glowered from her driver's seat, munching an Egg McMuffin. Waves of her discomfort washed across me for crowding her, but I told myself, "I am allowed to be here. She chose to park on the line, but I am not harming her."

Shortly thereafter, as I began my walk, I came to the death corner. So-called because of how many times drivers barged into that crosswalk when I had the walk signal. As always, I checked before stepping into the street. No surprise: along came a right-turner at full speed. I scowled at the driver. I nodded pointedly at my walk signal. He braked and gestured for me to go ahead. How magnanimous.

Which is when I caught a left-turner, coming from the other direction, frozen mid-intersection waiting for me to cross. That driver was not only about to hit a pedestrian in the crosswalk but was also running a red light.

So: I stopped traffic *with my eyes.*

As I walked away, I thought to myself, "Y'all don't mess with me. I had a tough week."

Day 247 of Isolation

When I pulled into the parking lot for my walk this morning, I caught a police car in My Spot! The patrolman was standing next to another car, speaking to the driver. I wished he had parked somewhere else to do his business. You can imagine my delight when I approached, and the officer rushed back to his car, hopped in, and peeled out. Obviously, he was on a mission for his job, yet I couldn't help but think, "Now I'm bending people to my will *with my mind!*"

Now, if I can make this work on my children...

Day 248 of Isolation

Wednesday's online schooling was brought to you by Les Schwab guest Wi-Fi. I ran into a curb while picking up library books and took a divot out of the rear tire that couldn't be overlooked. Not covered under warranty because there was no "bonehead mistake" clause. I guess we can call that $200 "tuition". Or would it be "overdue fines"?

As annoying as that was, it barely registered as stressful in comparison to everything else. Which was cool. And not cool. It was Covid Cool.

Day 249 of Isolation

We continued our suspension of Saturday walks in favor Saturday work day. This week's project was fall yard cleanup.

My daughter showed up in black joggers, snow boots and short sleeve t-shirt, accessorized with pink gloves, a fuzzy headband and a mint green gauzy scarf.

My son showed up in a hoodie, beanie, and gym shorts.

It was 30° F.

Day 250 of Isolation

Any lengthy discussion of quilts and 8-year-old girls would be incomplete without mentioning the time when I borrowed one of Mom's quilts to make a tent in my friend's yard. It worked great... right up until the moment when I took the tent down and found four rusty holes in each corner where I had put the tent pegs in. Only instead of tent pegs, I used railroad spikes, plundered from the train tracks where I was never, ever allowed to play. It's a miracle any of us ever reach adulthood.

Day 251 of Isolation

During our fall yard cleanup Saturday, I tackled the arborvitae with my hedge trimmers. I don't fancy trimmed shrubbery, but these trees block the view from my kitchen window if I don't slash them down to size.

Damien wanted in on the power tool action, so I let him do a couple sides. There was one branch on top that was too thick to slice through safely, so I left it there to behead later with my pruning saw. Damien said it looked like a mini Christmas tree up there, and he thought I should leave it. Jeff came over a few minutes later, and said, "Hey! It's like a little Christmas tree. We should decorate it!"

If you can't beat 'em, join 'em.

So here it is. I'm sure the reason that it is not yet decorated is that Mary did not overhear the conversation. I wonder how long it will take her to discover this opportunity to string lights and garland?

Day 252 of Isolation

Back on Day 10 (page 16), this isolation mainly affected students — before shelter in place orders and reduced wages. I asked for my friends to pray for the parents of extreme kids — thank you for your prayers!

We're still struggling — you've seen our ups and downs, but this is not only about us Ehlers. Just among my friends, just among the things they were willing to share, there were three suicide attempts, one drug overdose, one runaway, a handful of police being called, failing grades, holes punched in walls...

Now, on Day 252, this isolation has touched all of us. Pandemic life is not hard for only these parents, but my heart cries out to Jesus for them. The kids are hurting; their helpers are hampered by no contact policies; and the parents are at the end of their ropes most days. Or all days.

I'm so grateful for your prayers, because the suicides did not succeed; the runaway was found; the overdosed is recovering. The burden is still heavy, and I ask for your continued prayer as God brings these families to your mind. You're the best!

Day 253 of Isolation

Why is Fred Meyer out of Windex, and knockoff Windex, and all blue cleaning liquid? What does that have to do with Covid? I mean, I understand why *I'm* out of glass cleaner: because my daughter is trigger-happy. What are all the other people doing, drinking it? They realize the president is not a doctor, right? I thought we covered this...

Day 254 of Isolation

ADHD causes executive function delays.

Daze of Isolation

Impulse control is an executive function.

Impulses like bursting through doors during work calls or school Zoom classes or Mom going to the bathroom.

So, we lock the doors. Now, we carry a little key marked with red tape and our initial written on it. The other day I couldn't find mine, and I became convinced it fell out of my pocket on my walk.

No problem: I walk the same route every day. I'll find it the next day. Here's a picture of my walk the next day. Guess that little red tape isn't going to stick out as much as I thought it would.

TIME FOR A NEW KEY.

Day 255 of Isolation

Be honest: you try to coordinate your mask to your outfit. I suppose if you do that, you'll be expecting bonus points if your undies also match. I'd give you bonus points for that. On the honor system.

Day 256 of Isolation

Have you been feeling a little off? A little... out of step? I think I found out why! I messed up my Days of Isolation count around the end of September and I've been two digits off ever since. Of course, I went back and fixed all those entries. For the book. Well, and also because I'm a teensy bit compulsive. I'm sure you'll feel better now.

Day 257 of Isolation

Well, the day everybody knew was coming arrived. Washington is shutting things down again. How can I tell everyone knew it was coming? Costco's out of toilet paper again. The return of TPocalypse.

What's the same? No more restaurants, no more gyms, no more museums. It comes as a blow. We each had found some little perk that was helping us stay cheerful.

Mary went to twice weekly Taekwondo lessons, albeit with no sparring and a mask. Taekwondon't.

Every time it was my turn to choose a restaurant, I said, "Wherever: as long as I can go inside and sit down and be served."

> **Server:** Would you like another Diet Coke, ma'am?
>
> **Me:** Yes, yes, I would.

What's different? More things are open than before. I think the library, for example, will still be able to check out books. We're still allowed to gather with up to five people outdoors, so Damien's sanity saving daily football workout with his two buddies can still happen. Pools are still acceptable, so Jeff can do his sanity saving swims. Mary can still go out to play.

Daze of Isolation

What's also different is that this is not March. The days are not getting longer, the weather's not improving. It's the bleak midwinter and our holidays are hampered.

Jeff and I are not exactly on the same page with all of this. He keeps up with the news assiduously; I avoid it. He's very mature about it; I'm pouty and rebellious. I acknowledge that we face a very serious possible physical health threat, but we need to balance that against a very definite mental health risk. I asked Jeff if we could please participate in everything we are legally allowed to.

That's when he drove past the restaurant he chose last night and took me to Red Robin for my birthday burger. I don't long for Red Robin so much, and we had an Oreo milkshake instead of the sundae, and I can take or leave the singing. A Red Robin burger is our birthday tradition, and I just needed a dose of normal for my birthday.

I know you know what I mean. For reference, you and I still have until midnight tonight. It's like Fat Tuesday and Oktoberfest and Banzai! Don't waste it on TP hunting. #livingitup

Day 258.7 of Isolation

I ran out of energy to cook. Aaaand I guess I kinda didn't think those who brought me to tears mid-afternoon (aged 8 and 14) deserved a home cooked meal. So, I told them that supper will be "everyone fends for themselves." The only thing I made was sourdough bread, because it'd been rising for 24 hours, so I had no choice but to cook it.

It was a raging success. Nobody griped about "not liking this" and I wasn't so tired that I snapped at them. I thought it was funny what each person chose:

Dad: Sourdough grilled cheese, salad, bowl of cottage cheese.

Mom: Salad with tomatoes, peppers, roasted chicken, and Italian dressing, with three generous slices of warm bread and butter.

Brother: PB&J on fresh sourdough, salad.

Sister: Leftover pizza, with American cheese slice melted on top to replace the mozzarella she ate off it earlier. Bell peppers dipped in roasted red pepper hummus, leftover pumpkin bread from breakfast, Pear cheese muffin.

Tonight, I leave you with this: The reason bread rises is that the gluten in the flour makes the dough elastic. The yeast eats the sugars in the dough and gives off gas, which inflates the dough like wind in a parachute.

So, does this mean we are eating yeast farts?

Don't care — I ♥ bread.

My son calls these shower thoughts.

> **Trevor:** Yeast farts!!! and you killed the yeast and ate its last gas(p)!
>
> **Me:** I did not kill the yeast. Well, at least not before it aerated my bread into a lovely, golden-brown boule. I kill no yeast before its time...
>
> **Trevor:** So, you admit to killing *some* yeast.
>
> **Me:** Well, technically, I'm admitting to killing *all* yeast, but not before I've used it mercilessly for my selfish purposes. Then I guess I consume its carcass.
>
> **Amber:** I could get away with this almost never without someone crying.
>
> **Me:** My kids seemed delighted, and I'm trying not to let that bother me. Ungrateful wretches!

Day 259 of Isolation

High schools postponed fall and winter sports into February. Damien refers to his buddies by sport, saying this one's volleyball player, or that one's a soccer player. I told him that he and his friends will have to start identifying each other by what they *don't* play, like he's a non-football player. That offended him at first, and he insisted, "I'm a football player!" I pointed out that no one's *played* football for quite some time, though they are all on the team.

As a result of the significant increase in Covid-19 cases, the athletic director postponed football further into the spring. I told Damien that this is great, because now his non-football season won't overlap with his non-wrestling season anymore.

Day 261 of Isolation

Mary exploded into the bedroom this morning to start lobbying us for Today's Big Plan. She always has a Plan. Today, it was putting ornaments on the Christmas tree. Right. Now. Jeff distracted her by asking for another breakfast party. (Monday's Big Plan)

> **Jeff, satisfied:** I'm convinced redirection is the key with her.
>
> **Me, deadpan:** Yeah, you think that now. You're still young and vigorous. Talk to me at noon. Because that's what I thought Wednesday morning ("Let's set up the Christmas tree today!") and yesterday morning ("Can we put up the lights?").

Now, at 12:55 PST, our tree has ornaments on it. And all Mary's stuffies. She said we may take some stuffies off later — the ones that are scared of heights.

My daughter: Force of Nature.

Day 262 of Isolation

Overheard while Jeff and the kids were adding more Christmas decorations this morning.

> **Jeff:** Check this out! Mommy got this ornament when she was in 3rd grade. On the back, it says, "Ms. Vogel, 3rd grade, 8 years old."
>
> **Mary:** Mommy was in 3rd grade? And 8 years old?
>
> **Jeff:** Yep.
>
> **Mary:** That's just like me! *I'm* in 3rd grade! *I'm* 8 years old!

Ah, the magic of discovering what everybody else knows.

Day 263 of Isolation (My birthday)

Jeff shepherded the kids through buying thoughtful gifts, and he made breakfast. He was so harried by the process (and who could blame him) that he forgot to sign my card. So now I have a secret admirer.

Mary provided the party: Moose, Baby, Baby moose, and Olaf. Mary declared that she now sings, "...and many more" at the end of the birthday song. Whereas she used to sing, "and *any* more," which has quite a different ring to it.

Damien kept trying to reverse my numbered birthday candle cupcakes to make me a teenager again. He saw it in a video in which the birthday girl was 41. It took him a while to catch on that the trick is less appealing for a mom who is... ahem: late 40s.

Went to my birthday party at church: our church's first in-person service since shutdown. Governor requested us to not sing, so that was weird. But the *message* was excellent: PUSH...

- Pray
- Until
- Something
- Happens

After church, the family was very gracious to allow me to do whatever nutty thing crossed my mind. Highlights include sliding down a stair rail banister and sliding down an old-fashioned (i.e., metal) slide. They're so much faster than the new ones.

We also wound our way through St Mark's Cathedral labyrinth. It was intended to be contemplative. Somehow my children turned it into a racetrack. Joke's on them, because by the time we drove through Starbucks to redeem my birthday drink, they were both motion sick. So, I didn't have to buy them overpriced cocoa.

Day 264 of Isolation

This sh*t's about to get real. And by that, I mean that somewhere along my morning walk I stepped in doggie doo. I didn't realize it at first. I had driven home. Stopped in Jeff's office to say hello. Went into the kitchen to make sure Mary was on track with lessons. Left again to pick up the kids' materials from school.

Only as I was driving to materials pickup did I become aware of an odor. I thought to myself, "Wow, I'm not usually that fragrant after a walk." So, I guess you could say it was a relief when I found out it was something on the bottom of my shoe. Small consolation as I was cleaning all the footprints off my hall carpet.

Day 265 of Isolation

Mary wanted to do her math in her bedroom, so she could "concentrate." I told her to do it in the kitchen, so she wouldn't look up the answers in the back of the book. Yeah, kid — I had a math book, too. She sighed dramatically and agreed, but insisted on wearing her ear defenders, so *I* wouldn't bother *her*. The irony.

Day 266 of Isolation

What's on *your* menu for Thanksgiving? I bought a turkey, but I'm not making turkey. I bought a ham, but I'm not making ham, either.

For this holiday made weird by Covid, I think I should not be expected to make sensible meals. I made a turkey for my family in the spring: I can show them a picture if they forgot.

I told them that they could each add their favorite holiday dish to the menu, although I might ask them to cook it. Damien chose pumpkin pie; Jeff listed cheesy potatoes; Mary wants cinnamon rolls. Nobody said turkey, so we're having a yummy green bean and ground beef casserole called Taste of Home[15], and cheesy potatoes, and pumpkin pie. Cinnamon rolls for breakfast. That is all.

---

[15] https://trimhealthymama.com/ezine-homepage-december-2017/green-bean-casserole/

Daze of Isolation

WEIRDSGIVING DINNER

Day 267 of Isolation (Thanksgiving)

Mary and I strung cranberries and popcorn as an activity, and to decorate our accidental topiary Christmas Tree from Day 251 (page 173).

Mary: I'm catching up to you!

Me: It's not a race. I'm enjoying spending time with you.

Surviving Pandemic Motherhood on Diet Coke and a Prayer

Mary: It's a race.

Me: I'm going to slow down to spend more time with you.

Mary: I'm still winning.

Me, thinks to self: Me, too.

Day 268 of Isolation

Today is Black Friday; I'm not participating. The only appointment today is a Thanksgiving Zoom call with my father-in-law's side of the family. Each household will be serving whatever they want, so I chose a Round Food theme. So far, it sounds like we'll be having pizza, peas and carrot medallions, and pumpkin pie. It appears that we also like foods that start with "p." I suggested Oreos several times but did not have any takers. I don't understand it, either.

Day 269 of Isolation

I was too busy to write, because I was getting a spa pedicure. I'm not wearing sandals, of course, because of all the winter going on. That means my toes are secretly fancy. #stealthpedicure #selfcare

Day 271 of Isolation

Sat at Starbucks all evening with a Grande Salted Caramel Mocha. Well, I was scrunched in the front seat of my car with my laptop in their parking lot, because... Covid-19. Whatever: it was quiet. I had coffee. Longing for a bathroom compelled me to return home, but the children were in bed, so it was almost like Starbucks. What if I have Jeff wear a green apron?

DECEMBER

DESCENDER

December was the darkest month for many people. The weather was gloomy, the days were shorter, Regulations inhibited Christmas celebrations. People made the best of it: I saw several families meeting in parking lots with blankets and lawn chairs.

●●●●●●●●●●●●●●●●●●●

Day 272 of Isolation
Somehow, I managed to cram my twenty-minute workout into an hour and a half. It's 10:30 in the morning, but at this rate, I'd better start cooking now to be ready by dinner.

Day 273 of Isolation
I gave in and laminated the sign that we display for materials pick-up at the kids' schools. I kept having to print out new paper ones as they got wet or ripped to bits. Now, Murphy's Law would suggest that Covid-19 will end soon, and the kids will go back to school, and so I won't need the stupid laminated sign. Let's all laminate our signs.... About time Murphy did us some good.

Day 274 of Isolation
My sourdough was on the fritz. Two loaves in a row: flat bricks. I tried to be cool; took some deep breaths. I noticed some condensation in its jar, so I theorized that the moisture levels were off. In

summer, I switched from a fabric cover to a lid, because the starter was drying out. I went back to fabric and today's loaf was lovely. My sourdough needed his winter hat. Disaster averted.

Oh, wait — here comes the dried-out crust again. Gah! I now theorize that my starter mutinied because of irregular feeding. He is so high maintenance...

Day 275 of Isolation

When we were driving home from prayer meeting Wednesday night, Jeff pointed out the lovely, full moon. He kinda waxed on about it, if you want the truth.

> **Mary, changes the subject:** Hey! There's police lights![16]
>
> **Me:** Yep.
>
> **Jeff, stuck on moon topic, offers his best wolf impression:** Aw-oooo! Aw-aw-aw-ooo!
>
> **Mary, refuses to leave lights topic:** No, Dad — it's we-ooh, we-ooh, we-ooh [siren noise]

Day 276 of Isolation

I had a lovely nap in the afternoon, and when I woke up, we planned to order takeout. It was Damien's turn to choose the restaurant.

> **Me, via text:** I'm awake.
>
> **Jeff:** Ready to go when you are... D chose Jimmy John's.

---

[16] Police lights flashing in front of us; not in the rearview mirror. In case you wondered.

Me: I have a coupon for a free sandwich there.

Jeff: Excellent!

Me: Guess I should get dressed.

Jeff: Yep.

Me: Going to have to stand first. [Pause.] Sitting up now. Don't wanna' rush into anything. [Changes from robe to PJs.] Clothes are too much work. I'm ready.

Jeff: Come on down.

DRESSING FOR DINNER.

Day 277 of Isolation

I mentioned how weird it is to go to Sunday service and not sing. Is it fine with Jesus that I simply listen to the music and the message in the lyrics? Of course. In fact, he's probably delighted that I shut my trap and listened to something he said. Is it best for everyone that we don't reach down deep into our lungs and expel everything in there with gusto? Yep.

Apparently, I just miss the sound of my own voice.

Day 278 of Isolation

Jeff put on regular clothes, so I asked him if he was going somewhere special. He said, no — he was dressing for success. Where would he go, anyway? He was wearing an upscale polo shirt, spiffy jeans and leather sneaks, but that was still about three times as dressed up as the rest of us. Covid success.

Day 279 of Isolation

I got a checkup at the doctor's today, which is what now qualifies as a "dress up" event. Zippers, undergarments, a shower: all the things. Everything checked out fine. Assuming my blood work comes back normal. Or at least better than Jeff's. Except now, I'm annoyed because I have to climb out of my warm bed to wash off my makeup. Not sure how I'm gonna cope with real life again, though I guess I have plenty of time to figure it out.

Day 280 of Isolation

Daze of Isolation

2020... the year Christmas decorations at the mall include caution tape. When they say "abundance of caution," that must be short for "abundance of caution *tape*."

Day 282 of Isolation

Fun with High-Schoolers... Damien called me while I was at Fred Meyer today.

> **Damien:** Are you available?
>
> **Me, in the pasta aisle:** uh... For what?
>
> **Damien:** I have to do an interview for school with someone from a different generation.
>
> **Me, thinking grandparents would love a call from him:** How 'bout one of your grandma's or grandpa's?
>
> **Damien, pleading:** Mo-om, if I call them, they'll want to talk a long time. It's only a five-minute survey about drugs...
>
> **Me, disgruntled on behalf of the grandparents:** Fi-ine.

He chose me because he knew I had little experience with drugs, making my survey go even faster. So, I answered each question thoughtfully... slowly... and meticulously, taking pains to stop for all the many interruptions that happen in my world.

Day 283 of Isolation

Nobody's coming for Christmas, so lovely family who buy presents for my kids are sending and dropping off their gifts now. I can't fit them in my un-secret hiding place (my steamer trunk), so we wrapped them all today and stacked them under the tree. So far, I purchased a single present for my own family. Combining these facts, this put me in the surreal position of having all my wrapping done and almost none of my shopping. How totally Covid.

Day 284 of Isolation

Last night, we had to drop by Fred Meyer for one item. Kids didn't want to stop, so Jeff promised to run in "super quick" while we waited in car. A few minutes later:

> **Mary:** There's Daddy! He *was* fast. Uh-oh! He doesn't remember where we are! Mom — put on the flashy lights!
>
> **Me:** He was here a minute ago! He didn't forget that fast... [Gives up. Puts on hazard lights.]

As Jeff got in the car, I told him the whole story of why the flashers were on, at which point he confessed that he had forgotten where he parked. At least he's honest.

Daze of Isolation

Okay, okay — I'll tell you. It was whipped cream. We had to make a stop to have whipped cream for our cocoa. We had to make cocoa so that we could try out these cute, over-the-cup gingerbread man cookies the neighbors brought over for the kids. What? We're *somebody's* kids...

Day 285 of Isolation

I wanted to call in sick today. I'm not sick; just sick of teaching without a license. This day does, in fact, suck. Was there some subtle cue I picked up on that warned me it would suck? Or did I somehow make it suck by my attitude?

Nature? Or nurture?

Or do 285 days of this wear a person down to the nubbins?

Later that day

Somewhere between 0 and 4.75 hours of cherub melting down, I also melted down. I'm ashamed of some of my behavior. One could say anyone would crack after hours of struggling, and one would be 100% correct, but I don't have to like it. We haven't had a drawn-out event like that in a while — I was out of practice.

As soon as I carved out a moment to myself, I tore through the house on a seek and destroy mission. I could not stand the sight of anything that has been the source of conflict. There were several casualties.

I did not want to share my fresh baked pretzels with someone who screamed at me all day. I gave one to Damien and the rest are in our compost bin.

The artificial deadlines of Zoom classes and homework assignments wear me out so much that I couldn't stomach dough that needs to be fed and pampered, so the sourdough starter is also in green bin.

The bundle of sticks which decorated the corner of my dining room are a frequent target for flinging. Now in bin. They were too long to fit, so I had the gratifying pleasure of cracking them all over my knee.

I passed the rest of the day in our recliner. Total school accomplished: ½ of a science question, most of P.E. and two math problems.

In short, there's a party in the compost bin, but better to vent my powerlessness on those things than any person.

Day 286 of Isolation

Even though this week has been dreary, there were two notable spots of light.

1. Two days ago, the treacherous Whirl-away garbage disposal stopped mid-whirl. Flipped switch a couple of times: silence. As you may recall, garbage disposal repair = soul-crushing. So, it took me two days to work up the nerve to push the red reset button, lest it not reset. I turned it on with fear and trembling and behold! Whirling! Soul uncrushed!
2. My lab results from last week are in: cholesterol is down twelve points from last year! That'll give Jeff a run for his money. His physical isn't until January 6th, so that gives me some time to feed him lots of fatty foods. Oops — did I write that out loud?

In addition to these, there were many huggy hearts, comments, prayers, and texts. Friends are the best! There haven't been any more meltdowns, and we think we're seeing the beginnings of long-term progress. Those kinds of things happened daily before — now they are less frequent and shorter.

Day 287 of Isolation

Yesterday was better than the day before, trying to make today better than yesterday. I can tell God supports this initiative, because my McDonald's app offered me a free Egg McMuffin.

I've been gloomy as a baseline, so I'm about two steps from losing it at any given point. On one hand, what is *wrong* with me? On the other hand... Duh! Parenting! eSchool! Pandemic! Traditionless Christmas! Short, cloudy days! I S O L A T I O N ....

I'm not alone in this, and you're not, either. When my friend took her child in Monday because the child was making a suicide plan, she was thirteenth in line! At a children's hospital! It's dark right now — let us take care of ourselves and each other.

Day 288 of Isolation

Christmas is still two weeks away, but we already received three packages of pancake mix as gifts. The people have spoken! Breakfast for dinner!

Surviving Pandemic Motherhood on Diet Coke and a Prayer

Day 289 of Isolation

We used to do sporadic family movie nights, but when our state shut down, we made every Friday "Movie Night." We buy two medium pizzas for $12 at Papa John's, add some salad to make like we're competent parents, and settle down in front of a film.

The other day, the manager of Papa John's pulled Jeff aside to ask if we would mind being part of a test group for their new stuffed crust pizza. Uh... Does a bear poop in the woods? The manager said he would he wanted to make sure and reach out to all his *high rollers*.

That about sums it up for me: I operate at the level where $12 a week makes us High Rollers. Less than that, because Groupon gives us a 10% rebate.

So, this Friday movie night was an embarrassment of riches, because we got our usual two medium pizzas, and a bonus large stuffed crust. It was remarkably filling, because both children said they were full after only one or two pieces. Whoa.

Day 290 of Isolation

We take turns choosing movies and Damien picked *Home Alone*. Since I'm the only American who does not love Macaulay Culkin, the choice confounded me. I do not want to endure that film.

Then inspiration struck! We will leave the children HOME ALONE to watch *Home Alone*. Meanwhile, we will go on a date. Yes, it was only Christmas shopping at Fred Meyer, but it was *uninterrupted* shopping. Next, we put our items in the car, and went back inside to have Starbucks.

Because that's the way High Rollers roll.

Day 291 of Isolation

I explained to the kids Sunday that Christmas break won't be a bunch of lying about. Mom has put a strict schedule in place, complete with curriculum.

Movie night.
Every night.
Christmas movies thru 12/25.
Non-Christmas movies after that.
Test on January 3.
There was much rolling of eyes.

Day 292 of Isolation

I've never made sugar cookies or gingerbread men before, because of all the rolling of the dough. This year, our cousin gave us mixes for both types of cookies, so I could hardly refuse. And while I was flour-coated anyway, may as well roll out all the dough at once. By that point, I'm sure it could be referred to as high rolling....

Mary made sure to use each cutter an equal number of times, organized every shape on its own row on the baking sheet, and transferred them to cooling racks, also in their own row.

Not gonna lie: it's how I would've done it.

Following that, we dispensed three full packets of icing on *exactly*:

10 Gingerbread men

10 Stars

10 Christmas trees

10 Hearts

10 Stockings

10 Circles

4 Small stars

For the love of God, nobody tell Mary there were only four of the little stars.

Now, Mary thinks she owns all the cookies she frosted, and is doling them out with all the compassion of Napoleon.

Daze of Isolation

Over and above all that, we had the winter solstice, the Bethlehem Star appearance (rumored — too cloudy to confirm), and a surprise snowfall.... What we did *not* have was dinner. The cook was beat. McDonald's: 'tis the McSeason.

Day 293 of Isolation

A friend told me that it helps if you put "Christmas" in front of everything...

We're having a minor Christmas disaster. Every morning this week started with a #mommyfail. Monday, I remembered at 8:26 AM that I had a Christmas mammogram at 8:35 AM. Tuesday, I forgot a Christmas therapy appointment, which (ironically) caused a Christmas meltdown. Today we woke up to find we were out of one of our Christmas medications.

She was right — it does help! Better go fold my Christmas laundry, so I can take a Christmas nap.

Day 294 of Isolation

Does it seem to you like there are more houses with more Christmas lights up, and they put them up earlier? People are acting like they aren't as busy this year with parties and commuting and performances. Oh, right...

Day 295 of Isolation (Christmas Eve)

My kids' favorite pastime this month is rearranging the presents under the tree. One kid gets them the way they want it, then the other "fixes" it and vice versa. This is why I didn't label their packages. I wonder if either of them deciphered my wrapping code?

Mary's about to explode if we don't let her open something soon. I'm 'bout to explode if they keep bedraggling my bows...

Day 296 of Isolation (Christmas)

We had breakfast à la Pillsbury while we opened stockings. I do the stocking stuffers, so Damien laughed at me because I was so enthusiastic as I removed all the things I gave myself. What can I say? I got me just what I always wanted.

After that, we packed the car with kids, dog, and gifts and played Santa all around the Puget Sound. We met family on the sidewalk, in an open garage, under a bank drive-thru, through living room window screens, and under a heated gazebo. We threaded the needle between Washington weather (cold and rainy) and Covid-19 restrictions (cold and distant).

Day 297 of Isolation (Boxing Day)

Jeff was making plans to take our holiday decorations down when we return from upcoming mini vacation. Nunh-uh. Day after Christmas, buddy. Ain't no way I wanna come back, travel weary, buried in luggage and dirty clothes and put away hundreds of ornaments and 700 lights... He's lucky I held off until December 26 — I've started on Christmas night before.

Daze of Isolation

The dog was like, "I feel you, girl." She did not move off this couch the entire time.

> **Brian:** You know Boxing Day isn't referring to storage boxes, right?
>
> **Me:** It is for us.

Day 298 of Isolation

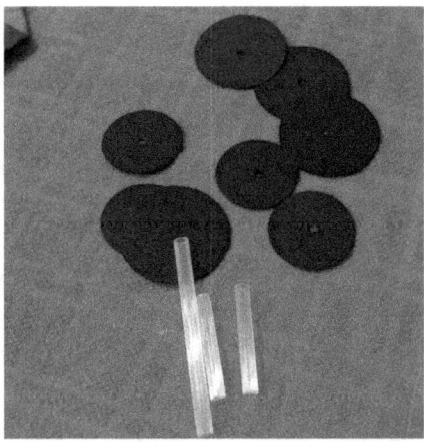

To round out my week of #mommyfails, Jeff and I overlooked giving Damien his main present from us. I also ordered it late, so we didn't even remember to give him a printed photo of his gift until today. Bag over head. For giggles, I made a somewhat-to-scale replica of the dumbbell and barbell set he's getting out of paper and straws.

Day 299 of Isolation

We took the scenic route to our hotel. We stopped at all the famous sites between Bothell and Blaine: Nike Factory Store and Nike Clearance Store. A place where we ask the kids to run inside: what's not to love? Everyone got new shoes, except me. Sniff.

Day 300 of Isolation

Semiahmoo Resort has little alcoves where guests can sit out of the rain, and out of our rooms. We found a room with couches to enjoy our complimentary afternoon cocoa, and I got antsy, so I brought a puzzle to work on. I thought if I started it, my people would gather around to help. But they went off to play pool. The dog napped nearby. It was so peaceful for a while.

Until it was nearing time for dinner, and I still was only 200 pieces into a 300-piece puzzle. Too far into it to start over, no way to move it to our room... By the time Jeff and the kids got back, I implored them, "Please help me. I'm trapped by my puzzle!" Jeff got a snack for hangry Mary while Damien helped me put the puzzle together. Though he hid the last piece, so he could put it in himself, as both children are wont to do. #typeAtroubles

> **Brian:** Why didn't you go for the Full Ahmoo Resort?

Day 301 of Isolation

Somehow, I think someone told Domino's that we're high rollers, because when I ordered our pizza, it came to $50. For one meal! How I longed for our home Papa John's.... And how I wish Jeff had told me a smidge earlier that Domino's has a matching deal to Papa John's. I managed to sweet talk them into accepting a $5 coupon I found on their counter. Which I promptly gave back in the tip. Oh, well. I rested better knowing my money would go to the dudes working the kitchen and not The Man.

Day 302 of Isolation (New Year's Eve)

We broke into Canada today. We were trying to go to the Peace Arch but took the turn for the border crossing by mistake. No passports. So, we got to tell our wrong turn sob story at least five times, and border patrol escorted us to the special holding area for sketchy characters and morons.

Surviving Pandemic Motherhood on Diet Coke and a Prayer

After that, we found the path to Peace Arch Park, which straddles the US/Canadian border. The inside of the arch reads, "May this gate never be closed." While the symbolic gate is open, the border itself is closed to all but essential travel. So, the Peace Arch Park is the only place relatives from both countries can meet to visit each other for now. Thus, on this cold, gloomy day, on a muddy lawn, families were having picnics. They conveyed the spirit of the Peace Arch in ways the letter of the law could not.

JANUARY

January meant back to non-school, which was as hard as it was when we left in December. However, we also got to back to our gym, swimming lessons, and church. The FDA approved vaccines and though our daily living was unchanged, a pinpoint of light could be seen at the end of the tunnel. If you scrunched your eyes up just right.

●●●●●●●●●●●●●●●●●●●

Day 303 of Isolation (New Year's Day)

I attempted to rectify a long-standing wound to my street cred. Twenty-five years ago, in Long Beach, Washington, I challenged my friends to go into the frigid coastal waters far enough to wet our heads. They gamely waded in to six feet depth. I waded in to about twenty-four inches, knelt, dipped my head in the water, and returned to shore. That's what I thought everyone would do, but they claim I cheated. Cheated! I never lived that down.

Until today.

At our hotel, there was a New Year's Polar Plunge. My strategy was to walk out until the 46° water went over my head and therein repair my reputation.

I only made it to my shoulders. The thought of having my head as cold as my legs was too much to bear. Reputation only partially repaired. Which is how it's gonna stay, because I will not be doing that again. Jeff and Damien, however, are planning to *jump* in off the end of the dock and swim back next year.

Happy New Year! We're off to a brisk start!

Day 304 of Isolation

It seemed kinda cruel to leave the count of days at 303, 304, etc., when so many were glad to kick 2020 to the curb and are trying to make 2021 a new beginning. That is the cold reality of the situation, though. Covid-19 is no respecter of calendars. So, we march on, but the end of the tunnel approaches.

Day 305 of Isolation

eSchool resumes for us tomorrow, and I'm nervous.

Transitions are tough in our house, so I'm trying to learn from the past. It seems like the first week or so of school or vacation is characterized by a lowering of my expectations. I start out somewhere around Pinterest Perfection and get beaten down to Plenty Good Enough.

What I will try tomorrow is to go voluntarily to Plenty Good Enough and save the kids and I some heartache. Wish me luck!

> **Patricia:** I shoot for adequate. Low expectations. Actually, I shoot for "done".
>
> **Karen:** You have too high expectations. I start at Plenty Good Enough but am willing to accept We All Survived.
>
> **Me:** I'm taking notes.

Day 306 of Isolation

Operation Plenty Good Enough was a success. There were several points today when I refrained from fussing or nagging, and let it go instead. Finishing math lesson during reading? Good enough. Stopping PE after twenty-five minutes though only 20% of exercises complete? Good enough. Skipping science questions? Even the teacher thought that was good enough, because he left a note saying they would do science tomorrow! Imagine how ticked I would've been if I'd gone to war over that! Supper was late, only 60% of the table cleared off: good enough. Calling it a day.

Day 307 of Isolation

Performance targets downgraded from Plenty Good Enough to We Survived, and even that is not promising. Eighty minutes into a meltdown; hiding in my room.

Later that Day

It worked. I gave up both my daily walk and my exercises and accepted somewhat less schoolwork (2/3 reading minutes, ½ math minutes, front side of worksheet and not the back, etc.).

We avoided meltdowns and had a satisfactory day. The sun helped. Or the bright clouds. Well, the lack of pouring down rain.

Day 308 of Isolation

I'm not sure what bothers me more: that people would storm the Capitol because they lost a hotly contested, thoroughly investigated election or that people were able to breach such a well-protected facility and do violence. Lord help us.

Day 309 of Isolation

First sourdough bread loaf of the year. What, you say? You thought I tossed my dough in the green bin?

I did toss it, and I was filled with genuine relief. For about a week. Then I started remembering all the warm English muffins, golden-brown pretzels, home-made hamburger buns, beautiful boules... Overcome with cravings, I decided that as soon as we got home from our vacation (January 1), I was going to ferment a new starter.

Surviving Pandemic Motherhood on Diet Coke and a Prayer

Which surely makes it my New Year's Resolution. Only January 7th, and I already checked it off. #overachiever

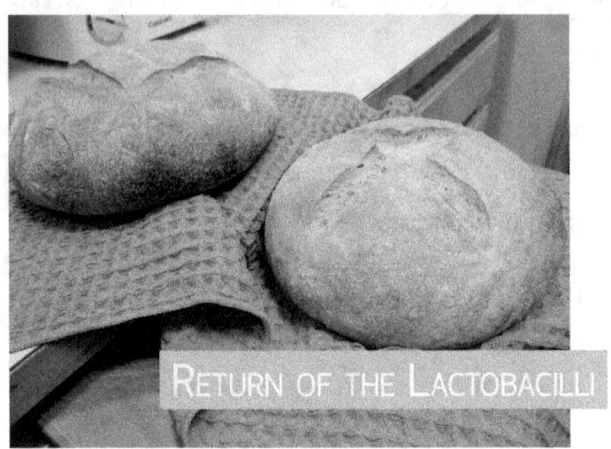
RETURN OF THE LACTOBACILLI

Day 310 of Isolation

There's no easy way to say this: it was a crushing defeat for Team Krista in the Cholesterol Championships. Jeff's cholesterol came in lower than mine by *three* points! In spite of all my efforts to spike his food with cream and saturated fats over the past month.

In the Cholesterol/HDL *ratio*, I did better than he. This is kind of like clinching my age group in a race. It's not nothing.

Team Krista will recover in the off-season and come back strong in the fall. We've got a bright future.

Day 311 of Isolation

What is the word for one morning of brilliant sun after record rainfall every day of 2021? Exhilarating. It was 28° for our family walk, but we were unfazed by the cold. Both children passed the time scouting ice on which to slip, slide, and skate.

Damien was crossing a driveway in front of a waiting car and decided to try a standing long-jump across it. He touched down on some black ice, so his feet flew out from under him. My boy landed square on his tushie so hard he bounced a little and his face mask went flying. He was fine, of course. (Youth.) The driver of the car met my eye, and we shared a laugh.

Wish I had it on video.

Day 312 of Isolation

Before Mary, I literally never purchased a roll of duct tape. I have no idea where the one in my kitchen drawer came from. Jeff, I guess. I married into duct tape.

I bought my first new roll in 2020; it disappeared in under a month in service of making a rolling desk out of cardboard boxes and a skateboard.

Today, when Mary was attacking my electrical tape to affix a pinwheel to her remote-control truck [a worthwhile endeavor], I introduced her to sustainable engineering. Consider, if you will, this roll of Velcro ties. They work as well as tape, and you can adjust as needed, like when you want to add another pinwheel to spin when the truck goes in reverse.

Science class: done.

Day 313 of Isolation

Our health club reopened last August, but I didn't go because they didn't open the childcare. Yet, when it stopped again in November, I felt so deprived. I can be fickle that way.

I purposed myself to not repeat my mistake. The club opened again today, and I was front and center, masked and squared away. It felt like a victory. Living life to the fullest! Getting what I pay for! Feeling the burn!

Bonus: it was inside, so it was dry. Always an advantage when the weather forecast includes a "*river* of rain."

Day 314 of Isolation

I was marching along my well-worn path, a little past where I found the abandoned underwear, for reference, and something seemed out of place. Oh, I know! The retaining wall that guarded the trail for twenty years is now part of the creek. Must be that 2700-mile atmospheric river of rain the forecasters keep yammering on about. Or the record 6.5" of rainfall that inundated the first twelve days of 2021. Or... the rocks got Covid.

Day 315 of Isolation

My trip to the gym the other day was partly reconnaissance:

Will the pool be open for Jeff? Yes.

Can I tolerate masked workouts enough to take Damien? Yes.

So, I offered to wake up early to take Damien this morning before his 9 AM class, and he was so happy that he spent much of last evening planning his workout.

> **Me:** *Dad's going to the gym tomorrow to swim, but he refused to take you.*
>
> **Jeff, indignant:** You said he had something else, so he can't go!

Daze of Isolation

Me: Only school. Besides [stares pointedly at Damien] *I* woke up early so you could go *before* school. At great cost to myself.

Jeff: ...and at no small cost to the one who had to wake her up...

Me: Just so you know who loves you.

Day 316 of Isolation

The school district maintains one master contact list, and we choose from multiple delivery methods, such as text, email and/or telephone. This same alert system handles snow day notifications, and I can't afford to miss those, so I checked all the boxes. I can no longer locate the boxes to uncheck them. So, here's how that math all works out during Covid.

For each notification (n), I receive one email, a text message, and two voicemails (home, mobile). Schoology will also post a notification on my phone.

$5n$

Double that because of messages students would ordinarily listen to in the classroom they no longer attend.

$2(5n)$

Then, if the announcement is particularly cool, Damien will forward me a copy of his email about it. If the info is especially significant, Jeff will forward a copy of his email about it. Jeff may forget he sent it to me and send it again.

$2(5n + (c * 1|2|3))$

When the robocalls happen while Jeff and I are in the same room, both our cell phones and the landline all ring in succession. Another perennial favorite: a text to notify me about an important email.

In short, I'm fully notified.

Patricia: I'm afraid to respond to this post ... might cause a cascade event!

Me: You mean like Jeff might tell me verbally about your comment? Because that happens.

Lorella: You still have a landline? (Yes, *that* was my take-away.)

Me: It had to be said.

Day 317 of Isolation

After months to think about it, I concluded that the things which are hard because of this pandemic were also hard before this pandemic. Those challenges are simply compressed and more intense, at times unbearable. I mean, my kids didn't "come down with" ADHD coincidentally with the start of the pandemic. I just had reinforcements before.

The Thanksgiving season made me realize that I am thankful for the extra time with them. My teen would otherwise leave before we woke up, returning in time for dinner. After which, he would lock himself in his room for the rest of the night to do homework. We are obliged to experience his grumpy worst, but we've gotten a lot more chance to enjoy his charming best.

We took advantage of the time with my 3rd grader to identify medication that works. We ended some therapy that didn't work and found some that does. Destructive meltdowns still happen, but they are fewer and farther between. We can at times head them off altogether.

But for this cursed isolation, I might have procrastinated on doing this parental work if they weren't home all day, every day, needing the work. Loudly. Sometimes, we're allowed a peek at all things working together for our good.

Day 320 of Isolation

My poor husband. He was settling in to take a nap (we take turns; he goes first) and I asked Mary to unload the dishwasher. She lost her... composure. Noisily. I lost my... composure, too, and Jeff had to take over. We also lost a baby gate, a decorative shelf, and a laundry bin. After Jeff got things calmed down, he took the kids to Costco to hunt up food for home and the food bank while I got my nails done, took a bath, and took a nap. It seems he did one other thing...

> **Jeff:** Uh... did you take the car out today?
>
> **Me, confused:** Yes. [I take the car out every day. How else would I get my soda?]
>
> **Jeff:** Did you realize that I cleaned and vacuumed the car?
>
> **Me:** You did? Wow — thanks!

Later, I went out again, to see how it felt to get a soda in a clean car. Felt guuuud.

Day 321 of Isolation

We had an 8 AM video call with our counselor — sorely needed, what with all the lost composure yesterday. It should've been simple: child goes first for thirty minutes; Jeff and I talk for the remainder.

But I forgot to put the Zoom link on our calendars.

And the Kindle went MIA.

Child doesn't like to use her Chromebook, because writing on the other person's screen is [wisely] disabled on that device.

We tried the old laptop, but we couldn't hear because the volume is blown.

We tried Jeff's work computer, but sound only comes through his headset.

So, we ended up using my phone.

That's the best we can do out of five laptops, two tablets, and three phones. Somebody needs to talk to the IT Department in this establishment. Oh, right — I'm the IT Department. In which case: our setup is fine, why are all these people complaining?

Day 322 of Isolation

I was making Egg Roll in a Bowl, and Mary asked to sniff the sauce.

> **Mary:** Ooooh! That smells yummy. Like Pop Tarts!
>
> **Me:** Pop Tarts?
>
> **Mary:** No — *pop tarts!*
>
> **Me, trying again:** Pop Tarts?
>
> **Mary:** No — *pot tots.* Er... Pot Hots.
>
> **Me:** Hot pots?
>
> **Mary:** Yes! Hot pots.
>
> **Me, somehow translating to:** You mean *pot stickers?*
>
> **Mary:** Yes, pot stickers! Can we make those?
>
> **Me:** How 'bout we go back to where you're happy with what I'm already making?

Day 323 of Isolation

Today marks the one-week anniversary of our brand-new garage door opener. Our old opener stopped working five days before school shut down last winter, and we were so proud because it had a worn-out gear, and we replaced it. All by ourselves! It only took all afternoon, much googling, and one visit to the neighbor with all the tools.

About the time we got the "second wave" of shutdowns, the opener conked out for good. Ungrateful so-and-so: after we gave it a shiny new gear, now it wanted a new circuit board.

We had a four-month standoff, in which we used the other garage door exclusively, before we caved and had a new opener installed, by professionals.

Now, it's all we can do not to replace the older one. It works fine, but the new one is way cooler. Restraining selves, but only just.

Day 324 of Isolation

There is never not a blanket fort in my house. In fact, she only dismantles them when she wants to build the next one. Because I keep a strict One Fort Limit. I tolerate the chaos and complete loss of pillows because the building process provides minutes of peace. An hour, if I'm lucky. Bonus: she likes to show it off by doing all her school Zooms in it.

Surviving Pandemic Motherhood on Diet Coke and a Prayer

Day 326 of Isolation

During today's sermon, our pastor compared unity to musical harmony — we don't have to be exactly like each other to unite and make a beautiful sound. He gave the example of a major chord: a c-note does not have to be an e-note does not have to be a g-note; different, but unified.

I looked at Jeff and said, "I call G."

Day 327 of Isolation

Mary was the last person in our house to experience a pandemic birthday. I'll be honest: I lacked energy or creativity for making it special. My first idea was indoor go-karting. Jeff and Damien wanted to race for first place, and I didn't want to be any part of that. Instead, I planned to give Birthday Girl someone to beat. So, I stayed behind her from start to finish, waving other people past me. For kicks, I slowed way down riding into the curves, so I could speed up coming out. Power out of the turns, Baby!

Even trying to place last, though, I got rear-ended three times by my son. It seems he "didn't hear" the part where the first and last laps were supposed to be slow. To be fair, "slow" isn't in his vocabulary.

I had a fabulous time watching Baby Girl hugging the corners like Speed Racer and rocking her maiden voyage behind the wheel.

Jeff and I agree that I should have stopped while we were ahead. Instead, I had the bright idea to make her birthday a Yes Day. This is a popular tradition in our house in which the parents say yes to virtually any request the child makes. Damien's Yes Days were wildly successful. This was Mary's first one.

We were ill-prepared for the depth and breadth of her imagination. By evening, she'd been surviving on one piece of pizza and a continuous stream of candy. She was glued to her screen for hours. She became an expert in telling us "no" by asking, "Can I not do that?"

Mistakes were made. For one, in the history of Yes Day, we never attempted one on a weekday. For another, in addition to Jeff working all day, he had a doctor appointment. I had to take the dog to the vet. Damien had to go to the high school to grab textbooks. I had to track down meds for the kids at 2 different pharmacies.

All In all, best we think of the go-karting as Mary's birthday and try to forget the rest. No problem. Forgetting things is something that comes easily at as I, ahem, "mature."

Day 328 of Isolation

Mary woke up far too early today and was revving up to a meltdown by 7 AM. Jeff dealt with that and came back to bed.

> **Me:** Wow — that was a lot faster than I expected!
>
> **Jeff:** Yeah, I'm trying a "Fifties Dad" approach. "You are not in charge, you can't do what you want until you finish what I'm asking you," and so on...
>
> **Me:** Fine by me. I'll try the Fifties Mom approach. "Wait until your dad gets home!"

Day 329 of Isolation

The photo on the front of today's paper hit close to home: a forty-nine-year-old woman lay on a hospital bed getting treated for Covid-19. In case people are still thinking Covid's an old person's illness. If any of y'all are saying to yourself that forty-nine is old, you hush your mouth, child.

Day 330 of Isolation

I don't mean to brag, but I just put my pajama pants on *both* legs at once.

Day 331 of Isolation

Way back when we got married, I helped Jeff sort through bags and boxes of his belongings to purge and organize them for our new home. Lots of things didn't fit with my decor goals, and he whisked them away to his office. When his company announced working from home due to the pandemic, he brought some of those things home. I made some space in my craft room/office for him to work. By August, he realized he liked working from home, and his employer allows it for his role. So, he lugged home another five boxes of doodads and a couple of pieces of furniture.

Today, I went in to move the routers, hoping to give the kids a better Wi-Fi signal. I ended up mounting them on the wall. Now I think I deserve to call that the "Data Center."

All my activity inspired Jeff to unpack his remaining boxes. Which necessitated removing the rest of my things to the closet. Now, his office is fully "Jeff-ified," which means a lot of shiny objects, many photos, every Valentine I ever gave him, and a dog bed. These are a few [hundred] of his favorite things...

Day 332 of Isolation

First day back at swim lessons for Mary. Well, first day back at any lessons! The YMCA installed a temperature self-check station, and I'm obsessed with it. It's like the grocery store self check-out, only *we* are the groceries! I wonder what happens if someone

Surviving Pandemic Motherhood on Diet Coke and a Prayer

presents with a fever? I imagine klaxons and flashy lights and someone rushing out in hazmat gear, a la Monsters, Inc.

Day 333 of Isolation

Finally figured out I can lip sync to songs in Sunday worship. My lips think I'm singing, but I'm not spreading my potentially-Covid-bearing cooties.

Also, I'm always on pitch, on key, and I sound like Lauren Daigle.

FEBRUARY

FEBRUTALLY

Vaccines were going into people I actually knew, and our hope grew.

• •

Day 334 of Isolation

Kinda overwhelmed. By reason of 1000 photos I discovered soaking on damp and moldy carpet in our office closet. We came across them as I was finishing up the Jeff-ification last night. We pressed every scrap of cardboard we could find into service as a drying rack in our garage. No biggie — it's only most of Jeff's childhood that took a bath. Gah! I suited up in comfy britches and a hoodie, as I spent the morning scanning the dry-ish ones. By noon, I needed a change of scenery, so Mary and I snuck out to Costco grab some fresh pillows. [On sale this month.] This was how I ended up in Costco in red velour pants and Birkenstocks. With socks.

But let's focus on the positive. On the *way* to Costco, I tied Jeff's record of four times around the traffic circle, and if that's not enough excitement, every bed also boasts a fluffy new pillow.

Day 335 of Isolation (Groundhog Day)

We need an animal for this pandemic. Like if he sticks his head out and starts coughing, 6 more weeks of Isolation... I nominate the Meerkat. Meerkats make me happy.

Day 336 of Isolation

I had to run Fred Meyer to replace our surge protectors in the "Data Center." There was some kind of snafu in which the Data Center tech [me] was twirling the old surge protector to unwind it. It was plugged in at the time. I was just wondering what that metallic rattle could be, when it gave off an alarming spark. The room went dark and all the system fans spun down.

Enough about that. After trying the puny Fred Meyer surge protectors, I had to go back out to Staples to find surge protectors designed to accommodate the chunky adapters for all the things.

I decided to take Mary with me to introduce her to the wonders of office supplies. Not kidding. On the way home, she said something snarky, then...

> **Mary:** Sorry, Mom, I was being sartastic.

I take this to mean that she is *fantastically* sarcastic, and I approve. I'm rather sartastic myself.

> **Lorella:** I too am sartastic. And adorkable.

Day 337 of Isolation

Have you ever wondered how many photos fit in one of those shoe boxes? 954. I found out because I finished scanning all the photos that got water damaged in the bottom of my craft closet.

Daze of Isolation

Me: You sure have a lot of pictures of the water tower by your mom's house...

Jeff: Of course. It was my muse.

Perhaps you're also wondering how I managed to find time to scan, date and label 1,000 photos in four days. Simple — I ignored cooking, grocery shopping, exercising, bathing, sleep, and calling someone to locate the source of the water leak in the closet. I dub this "The Ignorance Method," and it works for me.

Day 338 of Isolation

I had a caffeine sandwich.

First, a Diet Coke with my lunch.

Next, I had a coupon for a free Starbucks drink. It expired today. I couldn't let that go to waste, so I turned it into a Grande Salted Caramel Mocha.

Eventually: Thirsty again and it was time to go home. Another Diet Coke "for the road."

Day 339 of Isolation

As we covered previously, my data suggests that electrical devices *can* catch Covid-19. However, when the brand-new vacuum cleaner stopped sucking, that crossed the line! I was forced to crack open the manual. Come to find out, the tube was blocked.

The revival of the new vacuum inspired Jeff to apply the same solution on our old, dead vacuum cleaner. Thanks to significant dragging of my feet, it was still sitting in our garage. He dislodged a clog in the tube he described as a "hockey puck". A small rock, a Lego ice cream cone, a screw, and a tiny plastic turtle were all mummified in a snarl of dog hair. I am now happy to report two electrical devices recovered from Covid-19. Things are looking up.

Day 340 of Isolation

I love going to the grocery store so much that I make a list for the whole week, take an hour on a Sunday to retrieve and stow all those things, but strategically forget an item I need for Sunday's and Monday's dinners. To make sure I get to go back again Monday. Gah!

Day 341 of Isolation

Went to thrift store with child. No, we did not need an almost life-sized teddy bear, nor an eight-foot, neon rainbow, plush caterpillar. But she is allergic to leaving an establishment without making a purchase, and she only had $1. Looking at the bright side:

- They aren't loud.
- They aren't breakable.
- They won't hurt if wielded as a weapon.
- They aren't a whistle.

Daze of Isolation

Because the only thing she found that she could afford (before we discovered the 25¢ toy sale) was a shiny, 99¢ whistle.

That was a close one.

Day 342 of Isolation

In the process of reorganizing my craft closet, Mary came upon my stash of special stuffed bears. Like the one my brother made in elementary school and gave to me when I had my 3rd hip surgery. Or the one my friends had waiting for me after my 4th hip surgery. Or the one Jeff gave me in which I "stored" some extra hugs for 4-year-old Damien the first time I went away overnight.

> **Mary, picking up the middle one:** What's this one's name?
>
> **Me:** Maurice. But some people call him Space Cowboy.

Her new bear is now also named Maurice, and today's music lesson is complete.

Day 343 of Isolation

Our family experienced our first Covid-19 test, and I have to say, it was not as bad as the rumors led me to believe. I simply drove up in the car, handed them the signed consent form, and a delightful lady gave Damien a swab. I watched him swirl it 10 times in each nostril — didn't hurt a bit.

> **Sue:** The trick is shoving it up your nose far enough. I think they want you to touch your brain with the swab.
>
> **Me:** I hear you saying that I should help him jam it up there next time. On it.

Day 344 of Isolation

It took me the last three days to install an adapter that uses our electrical wiring for network traffic, so that I could give Damien a hardwired connection to the internet. He kept getting weak signal warnings during his school. The package said it was an easy install, which is often the kiss of death.

And it was. There were only two buttons, how hard could it be? Hard enough to seriously consider running a fifty-foot Ethernet cable through the office ceiling to his room. Said the woman who has never been in her attic or crawlspace, because: icky.

The instant that gorgeous green light of connectivity ignited, I rushed up to Damien's room to plug in his computer, aaannd....

Chromebooks don't have network jacks. So, I ordered a converter. Because that's what I wanted to do: spend some more money. At least it works now.

Jeff wondered how people cope when they don't have 8 years of IT experience and a computer science degree. I said I'm guessing they sit in the corner and cry and throw things, because that's what I nearly did.

Day 345 of Isolation

I'm experiencing a remarkable surge in productivity. I attribute this to my friend Sue's suggestion to replace Fix-it Fridays (too frequent) with Fix-it February. That appears to be "just right," because here it is, February, and I fixed broken glass in two wall-hangings, scanned 1000 photos, plugged my son into the network, and then...

I read somewhere that Habitat for Humanity Store will accept donations of unused siding, and even after 345 days, I'm still trying like crazy to make room for all my people:

Daze of Isolation

> **Jeff:** craft room-turned-office
> **Damien:** garage-turned-weight room
> **Mary:** buffet-cabinet-turned-craft storage

So, I piled fifteen 12-foot boards of HardiePlank into my 10-foot minivan, clamped it down with a tarp strap, and lugged it all to Everett. Think of all the space I freed up in the weight room! And then...

I decided I may as well build the shelving I've been meaning to add to the laundry room since 2003. Which was non-trivial because half that room is under the stairs, so the shelves have to be three different heights and... IKEA is out of stock on all of them. Home Depot: here I come. Phase One completed during Friday Movie Night; Phase Two throughout Saturday Snowmageddon. Bam!

I wish this level of activity could go on forever, but historical patterns show that it will peter out soon and be followed by months of lethargy. Enjoying it while it lasts.

> **Tiffani:** One day of work = 2 weeks of rest!
>
> **Me:** I like your math.

Day 346 of Isolation

8.5" of snow fell in the last 18 hours, so it's kind of like detention and being held in for recess around here. Petco and gym closed, swimming lessons cancelled, haircut place and McDonald's dark: complete change of Saturday plans.

However, I am undaunted because Midwinter Break has begun! I dreaded this storm all week, because I was afraid they would not cancel school. Why would they? We're already at home. I could not conceive of a way to entice my kids to sit at a computer while sledding was going on. Thank you, Jesus!

So, they passed the entire day on the sledding hill, while I finished the shelving in the laundry room. I went out for materials, and the driving was tricky in places: the snow was deeper than the undercarriage of my car, and most of the roads weren't plowed. Nevertheless, I motored along steadily in my minivan, passing several big, bad 4-wheel drive SUVs stuck in the ditch. I learned to drive in Alaska, and they don't declare snow days.

In short, school's out and everybody enjoyed their favorite snow day pastimes.

Day 347 of Isolation (Valentine's Day)

Jeff took me away to Cedarbrook Lodge for the night. I drug my feet a little — the prep for even one night away is daunting — but he persevered. This hotel has three buildings of rooms, each with its own living room, as well as the main lodge with lobby, restaurant, bar, and conference center. We whiled away the afternoon and evening trying out every seat in the house. It was like Where's Waldo, Ehlers Edition.

For entertainment, we enjoyed the same things we do at home, only relaxed and without interruptions.

Daze of Isolation

In the spirit of true love and Valentine's Day, I even let Jeff use the charger in spite of my phone battery sinking to 43%.

Day 348 of Isolation

On the way home from our Valentine getaway, we stopped at IKEA for a few things to use in the laundry room makeover. It was risky taking Jeff to IKEA — he's been in an expansive mood, and I'm lucky we made it out alive. He kept finding art that would "look great on our walls," and I was thinking, "How many walls do you think we *have*?" We've lived here almost 18 years: all our walls have stuff *on* them.

At 11:30, we entered IKEA, and he said we had plenty of time to reach home by 2 PM as promised. He's so cute. By 1:30, when we'd only progressed to the marketplace, he got a little... tense. You'd think he'd have learned by now to never tell me I've got plenty of time...

When all was said and done, our purchases fit in the car and so did we. We were only a little late, and best of all: I avoided a special trek to get all the things. And guess what? I found out that smallish

Surviving Pandemic Motherhood on Diet Coke and a Prayer

items only cost $5 shipping, so I may never have to go to IKEA with children again...

Day 349 of Isolation

Skipped all the things I was supposed to do (see also "Ignorance Method") so I could paint the laundry room. I hate painting — the prep; the clean-up; constantly teetering on the verge of latex disasters. I blunder through, though, because it will be so dreamy.

Damien was pressed into service moving boxes and shelves and washer and dryer. He helped wash walls, remove switch plates, and vacuum. Plus, he was good company.

He started to walk away when I was finally all set to paint. I told him it wasn't fair that he had to do all the hard work and miss the fun part. So, he suited up in Dad's old clothes and grabbed a roller. After about a half hour he said, disillusioned, "This isn't fun." Why not? I even gave him the easy walls. I said he could stop if he wanted, and he disappeared in a puff of smoke.

I guess we don't have the same idea of fun.

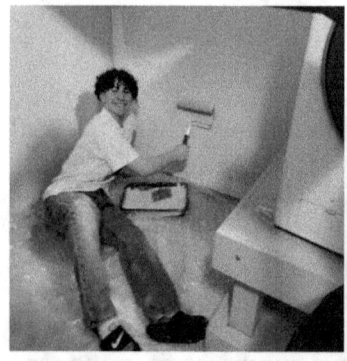 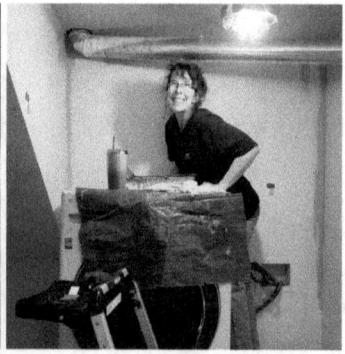

Amber: Wanna come help me pull out my washer and dryer and lay tile and paint? It's only a closet...not even a real room.

Me: uhh.... [Crickets]

Day 350 of Isolation

I *could* have gone to the gym, made a home-cooked meal, done my physical therapy exercises.... Instead, I finished the last scrap of painting, picked up a few items at Michael's, and reassembled the laundry room. By day's end, I was tapping nails on the finishing touches for the new, improved laundry room. We should probably name it something less pedestrian. How about "Laundering Center"? Jeff says it's so inviting that people will want to be in there, which was the idea. And while they are there, they may as well fold that load in the dryer.

I *could* show you the before and after photos, but I'm still waiting on a couple of bins from IKEA to arrive, and I'm sure you wouldn't want to catch the room in its almost-finished state. That'd be like almost-cooked bread. Gasp.

Jeff is about to explode, because he's not allowed to post his pictures either. Yeah, the power's kinda going to my head.

> **Tiffany**: High rolling and pulling rank on the hubby too? What's next?
>
> **Me**: Total world domination.

Day 351 of Isolation

I was distracting myself from my workout by listening to a parenting article. Child was displeased with her lunch choices and informed me in a way that displeased me. Soon, we were both yelling. Child screamed that I should leave, and I realized I should, in fact, take a breather, so I told Jeff I was leaving and got in the car. The radio linked up with my phone and continued the article I had queued up. A melodious voice drifted out of my car speakers, promising:

9 Ways to Discipline ADHD Behavior without Raising Your Voice.

Pfft.

Day 352 of Isolation

There he goes, in his red shorts and matching chili pepper face mask: first day of high school football. The protocols are all funky: players in masks, no spectators, short season. The coach refers to it as the "Covid Season." Yup. Nobody's complaining, though. They're overjoyed to play the game they love and hang out in person.

It rained the first day of Damien's very first soccer camp, and I was afraid the cold and wet would turn a 3-year-old off soccer. I persuaded him the rain meant he was going to be a *real* soccer player, because real soccer players play in the rain. He had a great time. Friday as I drove him to football conditioning in the rain, I recounted this story, and said, "I guess you're gonna be a real football player, too."

Daze of Isolation

That's probably what made me a mite teary as my eyes followed him walk off to the field for the first time, remembering the toddler, while getting glimpses of the man.

Day 353 of Isolation

When does isolation end for you? Or did it end already? Is it when you go (or went) back to work? When everything goes back to normal, or as normal as post-Covid life can be? When no one has to wear a mask in public?

My isolation ends when my kids go back to school. They are still 100% at-home learning. Our district was first to close, and I imagine it will be last to open. In the beginning, I wanted that for my sanity, but I'm rolling with punches by now. At this point, I want them to go back for *their* well-being. Not to mention the teachers', who seem exhausted. There are glimpses of hope: Damien has football, Mary has swimming. But still.

I'm a smidge optimistic, because our Governor offered financial incentives for school districts who draw up a Return to School Plan by March first. That being said, a plan could be anything. A plan could be, for example, "K - 1st graders go back by the end of March, add two more grades each month." We'd still be a couple of months away for Mary, and far longer for Damien. We shall see.

I guess you could call me, "Skeptically optimistic."

Day 354 of Isolation

In spite of school not reopening, Kids Church did! Mary was very excited. The kids' pastor said that she was looking forward to seeing everyone's legs. I'm sure she wasn't talking about my daughter, who treats Zoom calls like a full body sport.

Day 355 of Isolation

Made Yuletide Cheer muffins from a mix we got for Christmas. It struck me as strange to serve Christmas flavors in February, but needs must. At Christmastime, I was too busy making pancakes.[17]

Day 356 of Isolation

I was prepared for Monday to be hard, as the first day back from midwinter break, but it was fine. Tuesday, though. Tuesday was lying in wait to bite me in the butt.

Day 357 of Isolation

I spent hours Monday and Tuesday purging my files on my laptop because I was almost out of space, and I needed more room to stash photos from our phones. I managed to create almost 30 GB of storage! Yay!

Took me all today to upload the photos, only to find out that there were about 32 GB, and I was back where I started, with my computer doing weird stuff 'cuz it was gasping from the lack of hard drive space. Boo!

Then, something snapped off the inside of my wedding ring, and my ring was stabbing me bloody until I could pry it off. My ring fell victim to Covid. I'm down to a plain band to prove my title. Boo!

But! After months of languishing in my drawer, I revived my label printer. You can't imagine the backlog of unlabeled items that stacked up in its absence. Yay!

---

[17] See Day 288 (page 193), Breakfast for Dinner mandate.

Daze of Isolation

In spite of all the aggravation and bloodshed, Wednesday was still better than Tuesday. So... #winning

> **Amber:** You can label Jeff as husband in case being down a ring makes you forget.
>
> **Me:** Brilliant!
>
> **Jeff:** Awaiting my label.
>
> **Me:** Oh, it's coming. You can count on it. When you least expect it, expect it!

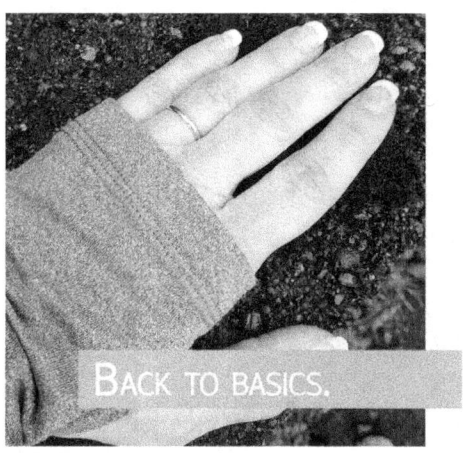
BACK TO BASICS.

Day 358 of Isolation

The moment you've all been waiting for: Laundry Room photo reveal. This is what passes for excitement around here. Photos delayed because one IKEA storage box arrived Monday; not the five I ordered. Luckily, I procrastinated instead of phoning their customer service, because the remaining four came the next day. No explanation. Which is like their assembly instructions, so I guess it's to be expected.

Day 359 of Isolation

Fun Fact, brought to you by my 3rd grader. Sticky Tack, commonly used to hang posters on the wall without damaging the paint, can also be affixed to your Chromebook to lock it shut. Simply place between keyboard and screen and shut tightly. Oh, the thrill!

What's that you say? The Sticky Tack residue won't come off when I open my Chromebook? Oh! What's that underneath the Sticky Tack? My microphone? My camera? My mouse pad, now stuck in the pressed position? Huh, who'da thought?

Sticky Tack: now a banned substance in the Ehlers Household. Happy Friday.

Day 360 of Isolation

What if I don't want any more difficult times?
Do you talk back to your fortunes, too?
Yeah, me neither.

Day 361 of Isolation

The pastor asked, "On a scale of 1 to 10, how controlling are you?"

15.

I admit I have a problem.

MARCH. AGAIN.

Sunday school was in full swing for Mary and Damien started playing football. We had fraternization once again. School drafted a plan to re-open, and our governor required them to include all students, and our hope came to fruition.

●●●●●●●●●●●●●●●●●

Day 362 of Isolation

I retrieved my repaired wedding ring, and I was able to jam it back on, so you could say I am now remarried. The Shane Company repaired it for no charge. I guess Tom Shane really is our friend.

Day 364 of Isolation

If I delete the Starbucks BOGO offer from my email *right now*, I will save myself $10, and over 1000 calories. This is important because President Biden vowed to vaccinate all adults by May 31st, but he made no promises about giving me a beach body.

Day 365 of Isolation

But soft, what light through yon' end of tunnel breaks?

Last Friday, our district's Covid Update declared that Mary would tentatively, probably, sorta' go back to class for one day on March 23rd. That would be Day 384 of Isolation, for those of you who don't keep a spreadsheet like I do. I waited until today to post this because it seemed like the Pandemi-versary would be a fitting day to share about her school re-opening. Also, I wanted to wait to make sure there were no backsies.

She will then have one day in-person the following week, one day the week after that, and the week after that will be Spring Break. Because they'll be worn out from that rigorous schedule.

After break, she will go to school two days per week and the remaining days will be so-called "Independent Learning" days, aka Parent Torture Days.

No matter: that's ONE and then TWO days every week that we can be off duty.

What about my other child, you ask? Middle and High School students are nearly invisible in this plan. With the upper grades moving around from classroom to classroom in infinite combinations, administrators contend they can't keep students socially distanced. At least he has football, and I'm not kidding even a little. "TGIF" in our house means "Thank God It's Football."

Day 366 of Isolation

Mary's math workbook has a regular feature called Puzzled Penguin, in which the penguin character confidently solves a math problem, but he's always wrong and students have to explain why.

> **Mary:** I don't want him to hear... [Covers Puzzled Penguin's picture with her hand, whispers:] He always makes a bistake!
>
> **Me, also whispering:** He must not be very smart.
>
> **Mary, sadly:** Nope.
>
> **Me:** Poor guy.
>
> **Mary:** [Uncovers Penguin's face, resumes normal volume.]

Day 367 of Isolation

Bought myself a special treat: New Sharpies! Fine Point *and* Broad Chisel Tip. All my people are kind of heavy-handed, so my old Sharpies weren't sharp anymore. They were Dullies. All better now.

Day 368 of Isolation

While I was out Saturday, I also purchased new weather seal strips for our garage doors, because several years ago, mice invaded our home. At the time, the pest control folks noted a narrow opening on the side of each garage door by which rodents might mount their attack.

I rushed right out and tended to that, as you can tell.... Naw. Like everyone else, it took a pandemic to motivate me. I gave myself several bruises trying to remove the old weather stripping, before a YouTube video showed me that it's screwed on. [Face palm.] It slid out in about 30 seconds after I found the screw!

On advice of same video, I sliced the old seal down the center for ease of removal. By the time I was done, it lay in tatters on my garage floor. Which is when I realized that the new weather seal will not fit in the door grooves. I bought T-end seals, and I need bulb-end seals. Only available by old-fashioned mail order; not on Amazon Prime. My long-suffering, supportive husband said, "At least you're doing it in the spring, not the winter, so the house won't be freezing while we wait for the new seal."

It was 31° this morning, but who's counting?

The shrews and mice, that's who. Because I'd made their 1-inch doorway eight feet wide.

| Karen: 🐁🐁🕳️🐀🐁

> **Me:** Allergic. Or should I say 🐘🐘 = 💀💀

Day 370 of Isolation

> **Mary, trying every argument to dodge her work:** It's not fair! Dad has to work, Damien has to work, I have to work, and *you* get to do whatever you want.
>
> **Me:** Uh-huh. So, you think I *want* to be doing third grade math right now?

She's lucky, because when her brother tried something like that, he got to do my "not work" until he cried uncle.

Day 371 of Isolation

Our pastor said Sunday that stress is the fear of not getting my needs met.

Word.

This came in handy, as my daughter declared today to be Scream and Not Do Math Day.

It was not pleasant, but I thought about my needs [Get Stuff Done] and I thought about how well my needs are always met by the Meeter of All the Needs, and we made it through. In peace.

All the math was finished.

And I got more of my stuff done than I thought.

Now if I can teach my daughter at age 9 what I'm still learning at 49.

Day 372 of Isolation

I got up one hour early this morning, quite by accident. I thought it was 7:45, but it was actually 6:45.

Whatever. Here's the real question: can I skip springing forward for Daylight Saving this Sunday, because I already did it today?

Patricia: Keep doing it. The hard part is behind you.

Me: You're suggesting I replace two days of getting up early with five days of getting up early? Because it's not like I can go to bed an hour earlier. I'm not sure if this math works for me.

Patricia: Just getting you into the groove...

Day 373 of Isolation

True confessions: I did not install the new rubber seal for the bottom of our garage door the instant it arrived. Too cold. When I did install the new one, it slipped in like buttah. Amazing what happens when you're not trying to force a T-shaped peg into a bulb-shaped hole. High on success, I attempted door #2 right away.

Quite experienced by now, I checked for the screw that holds the old seal on. I thought I found it, but when I removed that one the garage door started to come apart. Oops.

The second seal was not retained by a screw, but by pinching the channel closed at both ends. No problem — I applied about five minutes of strapping teen son to the pry those babies open and the old seal slid right out. Bam!

Day 374 of Isolation

It was the first of four Covid Season football games. It was almost normal, except for the masks and the temp checks and everybody standing far from each other. But there was plenty of screaming and taking pictures.

It was my son's first high school game — they're so much bigger than they were in Peewee! I started to tell him not to get hurt, but that's sorta dumb, since football's a bumpy and bruisy kinda sport. What I wanted to say is "don't break or die," but that would've put a damper on the mood. I try to pretend I'm chill. In the end, I said,

"Have a good game," and I told Jesus the rest. He did great; they won; nobody got hurt (TY, JC). Now we just need to do that three more times.

Day 375 of Isolation

The plot thickens here in Washington state! Governor announced that he requires all districts to offer in-person classes for K-12 students, two days per week, by April 19th. Shortly on the heels of our district superintendent allowing elementary schoolers, but not secondary students, back to school. Putting together several events over the past month, he was giving fair warning, "We're giving you vaccines, we allocated $2.6 billion, now make it so."

Day 377 of Isolation

Our living and dining rooms were overtaken by another in Mary's continuous string of blanket forts. She started it Sunday and is adding to it daily. I'm calling it the Winchester Fort, after the late Sarah Winchester's mansion, "renowned for its size, its architectural curiosities, and its lack of any master building plan."[18] But are you hearing what I'm hearing? My dining room is out of order: I don't have to cook!

Day 378 of Isolation

Lordy, Lordy, look who's... 15! Seriously, 15 seems so much older than 14. I got on the leg press machine right after Damien today. It was galling how much weight I had to remove. I thought it might work better if I went first. So, I wouldn't have to admit how much

---

[18] https://en.wikipedia.org/wiki/Winchester_Mystery_House

Daze of Isolation

weight he added, but then we'd both know how little I can press. Granted, I'm doing single leg presses, but still.... Somewhere between ages 3 and 15, he got way stronger than me.

Day 379 of Isolation

While the loss of life is finally going down in Washington, the loss of equipment in the Ehlers Household spiked sharply today, as we said goodbye to both a trusty laptop and my aged Pontiac Sunfire. The computer was outdated, and its main value was to prevent me traipsing all the way upstairs to use the newer one. Jeff has wanted to upgrade it for months.

> **Jeff, voice dripping with faux disappointment:** I guess this means we'll have to by a new one.
>
> **Me:** I'm not replacing this.

The car's blue book value is about 2.7¢ and, since Jeff is no longer commuting, we don't need a second vehicle most days. Training myself to share this late in our marriage will be a shock to the system. Jeff may be stuck at home a lot.

Day 380 of Isolation

We had actual visitors in our home! Jeff's dad, his wife, and her sister were the first among our family to be vaccinated, so they came over, and they brought lunch! Everybody was so excited. I even vacuumed. It's not like we had many visitors before [Introvert Mom], but it's different when hosting visitors is a crime.

Jeff and his dad traded puns, as per family tradition. A few hours after they left, Mary asked Jeff to make sure her Barbies didn't drive away while she was having supper. Jeff said, "Sure, I'll keep an eye on them."

A few minutes later, Mary and I looked over. There was a sticky note on Barbie's motor home with a large capital "I" written on it. Unsatisfied with a single pun, he then moved to the letter "I" to the lid of a jar.

> **Me, chuckling in spite of myself:** That's pretty good.
>
> **Jeff:** Must be because Dad came over today.
>
> **Me:** Yeah, we'll have to tell him that his spirit is lingering on in our kitchen.
>
> **Jeff:** The Pun-o-sphere.
>
> **Me:** Or perhaps, the Punish-sphere.

We were still worked up from all the human contact.

Day 381 of Isolation

This season has been characterized by mild, but grinding deprivation, punctuated for many by shocking loss — of life, of business, of jobs. But who's winning Covid-19?

- Netflix

- Animated feature films — socially distant by nature.
- Zoom. Who even heard of them before?
- Utilities companies. Well, they may not be getting more money overall, but they're getting more of my money...
- e-tailers
- Restaurants with online ordering. Our Red Robin has twenty-two parking spots for takeout customers.
- Grocery stores. (Fred Meyer, I'm looking at you...)
- Buildings! Lots of renovating while they're on hiatus. My McDonald's recently started their remodel: Merry Christmas to me!
- Dogs: never alone again.

And you and me. We're winning, because we made it. We're not in the clear yet, by any means. CDC and government officials are still pleading with us to keep wearing masks and washing and staying distant. Yet the signs of life are appearing with increasing frequency, and if you're reading this, you survived, and that's winning.

Day 382 of Isolation

My pandemic by the numbers:

79 crossword puzzles

9 jigsaw puzzles

470 email threads from the school about Covid

552 face masks sewn

169 pounds of flour, an estimate based on my memory and what my scale tells me.

3% increased utilities costs with 4 people home. Seemed like this would be higher. Perhaps I saved money from all the days I didn't bathe.

392 containers salted caramel crunch yogurt
337 gallons of Diet Coke.

> **People:** She's kidding about the Diet Coke, right?
>
> **Me:** Sure. Let's go with that.

Day 383 of Isolation

Today, Mary got on a school bus for the first time in 383 days, marking the beginning of the end of our isolation.

The schools are required to let Damien go back by April 19th, and I told him that he should not expect it one second before their deadline. Kinda like how teenagers do homework.

This pandemic thrust each of us into roles we never imagined and wouldn't have chosen.

Students all got kicked off campus and their classes turned into correspondence courses. Parents became para-educators. Teachers became audio visual experts, or wished they were.

Bus drivers became tech support, meals on wheels, and book-mobiles.

Pastors became televangelists.

Stay at home moms' workplace got invaded; career moms and dads suddenly had loud and disruptive office mates.

Clerks, city bus drivers, and other essential workers found themselves on the front lines of a war against an invisible attacker. Soldiers are delivering vaccines.

We all became amateur epidemiologists.

Now, we're all gonna try to squeeze back into our former roles. Tomorrow will be just... A day. Peace out, my friends.

Daze of Isolation

EPILOGUE

We made it. The kids are still happy to be back at school, even part-time, with masks, with weekly Covid tests and daily temperature checks. We're still getting excited as each restriction lifts and more places open their doors.

●●●●●●●●●●●●●●●●●●●●

Day 398 of Isolation

I suppose you're wondering what a stay-at-home mom does on the first full day of school in over a year. She takes the day off. I went for a walk, picked up the groceries, put them away...

... And took a bath, and lay reading for a couple of hours and went out to McLunch. For dinner, we had whatever each person could find in the fridge.

It was magnificent.

Day 412 of Isolation

Got my first dose of vaccine. I feel good. I feel half immune.

Day 413 of Isolation

Jeff tells me that they have so-called Vaccination Vacations. You fly to Maldives, for example, and they give you your first dose when you deplane. You frolic in the waves for two weeks, and then get your second dose. We did very nearly the same thing, because we trekked to sunny Arlington, and we also got our first dose at the airport. Exactly the kind of Vaccination Vacation that a Pizza Parlor High Roller would take.

Day 422 of Isolation

I'm up at 2:38 AM: may as well sign up for our 2nd vaccine shot. Sometimes insomnia pays off.

Day 425 of Isolation

Jeff set out the tax documents to work on our return tonight. He used to finish it about 6.8 hours after we received the last of our paperwork. This goes to show how the pandemic took its toll on us.

I can relate. I used to have a home cooked meal on the table every night, bank accounts balanced, house and car spotless, yard trimmed, well-groomed self and children.... I can't even type that with a straight face. Totally lying. Well, those things happen occasionally, just never, ever all at once.

Day 429 of Isolation

Got my 2nd vaccine dose today. I feel... sluggish and tired. But no more than usual.

Day 443 of Isolation

New math: 2 shots + 2 weeks = 0 Masks. As of 10:56 a.m. PDT, the CDC, Costco, and LA Fitness say I don't have to wear a mask anymore. I hope the other places I go will soon agree. Like Fred Meyer. (I don't go very exciting places.)

Day 483 of Isolation

Our governor lifted all restrictions in Washington, so ¾ of our family can move freely about the earth. We can breeze in and out of businesses and church and our health club. There's a single 5½"-by-7" fabric reminder that we're still in a pandemic, and Mary has to wear it at camps and indoors. We keep our masks near to hand still. The Delta variant looms, but I have a nice spot marked out in the sand, where I can bury my head as needed.

●●●●●●●●●●●●●●●●●●●●

I hope you enjoyed reading this book as much as I enjoyed writing it! If you did, I would greatly appreciate a short review on Amazon or your favorite book website. Reviews are crucial for any author, and even just a line or two can make a huge difference.

THE FUN DOESN'T HAVE TO END HERE!

Subscribe to our email list at kristaehlers.com, and get "The Lost Daze," an add-on to *Daze of Isolation* only available to subscribers. You can also follow Krista on your favorite social media site.

Website: kristaehlers.com
Facebook: facebook.com/kristaehlers.author
Instagram: @krista.ehlers

ABOUT THE AUTHOR

Krista Ehlers is a retired IT specialist and web developer, a former foster parent, and now adoptive mom of two. She is an experienced trainer, public speaker and comedian, and her passion is to lighten the load of other mothers by sharing her story with transparency and humor. She lives with her husband, children, and labradoodle in the Pacific Northwest, in a state of mostly happy chaos.

www.ingramcontent.com/pod-product-compliance
Lightning Source LLC
Chambersburg PA
CBHW072048110526
44590CB00018B/3090